Fifty Ways to Find a Lover

**Proven techniques
for finding
someone special**

Fifty Ways to Find a Lover

Proven techniques for finding someone special

Sharyn Wolf

with Katy Koontz

BOB ADAMS, INC.
PUBLISHERS

Published by Bob Adams, Inc., 260 Center Street, Holbrook, Massachusetts, 02343.

Printed in the United States of America.

ISBN: 1-55850-901-1

ACKNOWLEDGMENTS

Grateful thanks go to: Linda Antoniucci for her support; Stacey Winnice for her invaluable advice and zeal; Tony Cennamo for helping to get things started; Kathleen Spivack, Nancy Nowak, and Barbara Holder for their lessons about heart; Laura George, Mindy Marshall, Donna Zerwitz, Erica Wilton, Diane Langone, Cindy Morris, David Sparr, Daryl Sherman, and Carol "The Hornet" Fredette for listening; and Leon Maleson for his endless patience. Much love and thanks to Debra Wolf and Michelle Wolf, for legal advice and encouragement, and to my parents Norma and Milton Rubin. Special thanks to Jeff Herman, for everything, and to Brandon Toropov, who pulled it all together with such grace. For their ideas and support, thanks are due to Mimi Abramovitz, Roselle Kurland, Joel Walker, Bob Salmon, and the staff of the Hunter School of Social Work for their ideas and support. Finally, heartfelt thanks to the hundreds upon hundreds of people who took the workshop that formed the basis of this book. Without their wisdom, willingness to share, and unbounded enthusiasm, this book would not have been possible.

S.W.

I would like to thank the late Luis Sanjurjo for his encouragement and support; our editor Brandon Toropov, not only for his fine editing, but also for his unfailing sense of humor in a project that demanded one; and my husband Steven Friedlander, my parents Donald and Betty Ann Koontz, and all my single and not-so-single friends alike who faithfully rally when needed most.

K.K.

Dedication

This book is dedicated to Jamie Jaffe and Ross Klavan.

Contents

*Introduction/*17

Chapter 1:
Carry a Conversation Piece/19

Chapter 2:
Give People Your Card/23

Chapter 3:
Discover How to Make Yourself Feel Desirable/27

Chapter 4:
Tell People You're Interested in Dating/30

Chapter 5:
Learn to Type Shift/34

Chapter 6:
Identify Where You Get Stuck Most Often/38

Chapter 7:
Give Someone a Second Chance/43

Chapter 8:
Make a Wish-Need List/47

Chapter 9:
Don't Take Yourself Too Seriously/50

Chapter 10:
Practice Initiating Conversation/54

Chapter 11:
Establish Credibility Early /59

Chapter 12:
Make Your Imagination Your Asset/63

Chapter 13:
Find Places Where You're Comfortable Going Alone/67

Chapter 14:
Learn a Few Good (Clean) Jokes or Tell A
Great Story/72

Chapter 15:
Make New Friends of Both Sexes/75

Chapter 16:
Create a Buddy System/79

Chapter 17:
Learn to Transfer Your Skills/82

Chapter 18:
Buy Every Singles-Related Publication You Can Get
Your Hands On/85

Chapter 19:
Get on Every Singles Mailing List You Can/88

Chapter 20:
Walk Your Pet (Borrow One If You Have To)/91

Chapter 21:
When Going to Bars, Plan Ahead/94

Chapter 22:
Browse Through the Apparel Department (for the
Opposite Gender) at a Classy Retail Store/97

Chapter 23:
Spend time in Bookstores, Video Stores,
and Libraries/100

Chapter 24:
Go to a Trade Show, Convention, Auction, or Sale/103

Chapter 25:
Learn to Work at Your Own Level of Comfort/105

Chapter 26:
Get Out of Your Rut/108

Chapter 27:
Look Around Your Office/112

Chapter 28:
Learn the Art of Short Talk/116

Chapter 29:
Do Errands in the Evenings or on Saturdays/118

Chapter 30:
Tell Yourself You're Out of Town/120

Chapter 31:
Don't Be Afraid of Failure/123

Chapter 32:
Learn How to Take a Line/127

Chapter 33:
Throw a "Non-Significant Other" Party/130

Chapter 34:
For Women Only/132

Chapter 35:
For Men Only/136

Chapter 36:
Take a Class/138

Chapter 37:
Attend Weddings, Reunions, Alumni Functions, and
Family Gatherings/141

Chapter 38:
Join a Professional Organization/145

Chapter 39:
Join a Health Club or Take Up a Sport/147

Chapter 40:
Spend Time in Art Galleries and Museums/150

Chapter 41:
Take a Fabulous Vacation (Especially If It's Designed
for Singles)/153

Chapter 42:
Learn How to Flirt/156

Chapter 43:
Send Someone a Drink/160

Chapter 44:
Do Some Reality Testing/163

Chapter 45:
Make the Call/166

Chapter 46:
Learn to Ask for Less and Get More/171

Chapter 47:
Simply Smile/175

Chapter 48:
Read the Personals and Place an Ad/178

Chapter 49:
Answer an Ad/182

Chapter 50:
Find Out About Dating Services and Consider Using
One/187

Epilogue:
Staying Motivated/192

Introduction

An attractive man sits at the bar of his favorite Italian restaurant, having a drink while waiting to be called for his table. He will be eating dinner alone--again. A woman enters and takes a seat near him. He notices her, finds her appealing, and smiles briefly at her. She returns his smile. He wonders if she is meeting someone . . . or if she, too, is planning to eat alone. He decides he really wants to meet her--but an hour later she is still sitting alone, and so is he.

A woman working in a large office building repeatedly encounters the same man in various locations: the elevator, the lobby, the taxi stand outside. One morning, she nods at him and says hello. He smiles and greets her politely. Nothing else happens. They go to their separate offices. He doesn't wear a wedding ring, but the woman knows from experience that he might be married anyway. She'd like to get past hello, but she's afraid he'll turn out to be happily married and the father of a couple of teenagers. By the time she works up her nerve again, she thinks, he just might be. She does nothing.

A young accountant hasn't had a date in six months. Her friends have exhausted all their prospects for her; she hates going to singles bars; she doesn't feel anything special for the men who work in her office. On most nights, she comes home from work and reads science fiction novels. Once in a while, she might go out alone--to an art museum, her health club, or to shop--but she never sees men she wants to meet. If approached by someone she doesn't know, she automatically acts cold and distant, even if the person is only asking for directions or for the time of day. She realizes one night, as she brushes her teeth before going to bed, that she is extremely tired of being alone.

Why do so many bright, interesting, good-looking people spend so many Saturday nights watching late night movies all by themselves?

It's tempting to put the blame on demographics, bad

luck, low energy levels, or even our jobs, but these aren't the real culprits. The reason so many people stock up on Campbell's Soup for One is that they haven't learned the art of meeting others.

The good news is that meeting people is not an innate ability that some people excel at and others can never master. Meeting people is a skill, and just as with playing a good game of tennis or successfully programming a computer, you can learn how to do it if you approach it step by step.

First, though, you have to realize that you have the power to take control of your situation. Your future social life is *not* up to fate. It's up to you. When you stop to think about it, it really is remarkable how many people put countless hours and unceasing effort into their careers--and then leave their personal lives to chance! Rationalizations like, "It wasn't meant to happen," "That's just the way my life goes," and "There's probably a good reason for things turning out this way," simply wouldn't cut it if one were assessing career progress. Why are these platitudes so common when the issue is how to have a happy social life?

Life doesn't have to be disappointing, frustrating, or lonely when it comes to romance. Honest. But to make a change, you have to begin by forgetting about chance, about timing, about chemistry, about affairs that were "meant to be"--in short, about all the ideas that take the matter of meeting someone out of your hands. You are in control, and no one else.

This will become clearer to you as you make your way through this book. The invaluable techniques that are outlined here also form the basis of a successful workshop for singles that has been helping people get out and meet other eligibles for over four years. Over the years, participants in the workshops contributed advice based on their own experience, and these tips have been incorporated, as well.

The steps you're about to learn work, no ifs, ands, or buts. They've worked for the innumerable people who've taken the workshops--from the lean and mean to the balding and bulging--and, if you give them a chance and keep an open mind, they'll work for you, too.

So. Take a deep breath, tell yourself you're worth the effort, and get started.

CHAPTER 1:
Carry a Conversation Piece

A conversation piece is something unusual and interesting that can help you smoothly negotiate the awkward first stages of meeting someone. In other words, it's an object people will notice and ask you about. It's also something *you* can use to initiate conversation. It gets a dialogue going without sounding like a come-on.

A conversation piece *is*: a book with a provocative title; a travel brochure for Tibet; a roller skate key worn on a string around your neck.

A conversation piece *is not*: a tee-shirt that reads, "So Many Men, So Little Time"; any printed matter about a swinging singles weekend; a bottle opener worn on a string around your neck.

The right item can solve a number of important problems that often face single people. It gets you noticed; it makes you more approachable; it makes approaching other people easier; and it makes it easier to keep communication going once things get started.

Promising encounters are often brought to a premature halt because of the awkwardness the participants feel in trying to "make conversation." Here's an example:

> He: Nice day, huh?
> She: Yeah. It is. It *is* a nice day.
> He: Yeah. Sure is.

It's hard to imagine anything interesting resulting from that exchange, isn't it? Now compare an equally brief conversation opening that benefits from the presence of a conversation piece:

He: I see you're reading *The Book of Questions.*
She: Oh, it's wonderful. Have you read it?
He: No; tell me about it.

Vinnie, a weightlifter, bought the book *When Bad Things Happen to Good People* and took it with him to read on a long bus trip he'd planned. As he boarded the bus, he noticed a woman who looked interesting, and sat in the opposite row. He began reading the book, but had not even gotten through the first few pages when the woman leaned over and said, "That looks interesting. What's it about?" "Psychology," replied Vinnie. They ended up talking for the rest of the bus ride--*but the subject of the book never came up again!*

When Sarah bought *The Man Who Mistook His Wife for a Hat,* she had nothing more in mind than reading a book that had gotten some excellent reviews in her local newspaper. But strange things started to happen as she carried it with her from place to place. Everywhere she went, people came up to her and asked about it! Sarah finished the book (which lived up to its reviews, by the way) in record time-- but she still carries it around whenever she wants to meet interesting people.

Sarah's choice is a particularly good example of a classic conversation piece. The book not only carries that strange, unforgettable title, but is also designed in such a way that the cover demands attention from some distance. A good conversation piece should be able to attract notice and interest from across a room. (Once you find one, then, you shouldn't clutch it tightly to your body or keep it hidden away in your bag or briefcase. Take it out and get noticed!)

Conversation pieces don't have to be books, of course. The only limits to what you can use to get yourself noticed are good taste, a little common sense, and your own imagination.

Freddie's friends at work threw him a fortieth birthday party, and gave him a pin that read, "Oh No! Four-Oh!" He forgot to take it off when he left work, prompting a woman on the bus to smile and ask him, "Red-letter day for you today?"

Jody is studying Nepalese. She made some flash cards to take on the subway during her long ride to work so she could brush up on her vocabulary. She often spends more time talking to people who ask her about the cards than she does memorizing words!

Tony is an amateur astronomer who sets up his telescope on busy street corners during the summer months. For a quarter--and a little conversation--he'll show passersby the moons around Jupiter.

Alice often wears a sweatshirt with a foreign phrase emblazoned across the front. It's happened time and time again in just about any social setting: someone interesting will walk up to her, smile, and ask her to define the phrase!

The possibilities are endless. You might wear a baseball cap or an old college varsity jacket. If you play an instrument, you might carry the case with you. (Saxophones are particularly noticeable, though a bit cumbersome on a crowded subway!) If you carry a beeper, you might even set it to go off "accidentally," then turn to the person next to you and remark casually, "Gee, it doesn't do that for everyone!"

Once the great opening has been made, don't stop there. If someone compliments you on your red suspenders, don't just say thank you and stare back at the person blankly. You might say where you got them, or that you always wear them on Wednesdays, or why they're your lucky suspenders. Keep the exchange going; keep the tone pleasant, friendly, and light.

And above all, don't be so intent on your own conversation piece that you don't notice the conversation pieces other people may have!

While Alan was having lunch in a diner, two women walked in and sat next to him at the counter. The one closest to him put a book next to Alan's plate. Alan didn't want to interrupt, and said nothing until the two were getting ready to leave. Finally, he summoned up his courage and said, "Excuse me, but I couldn't help noticing your book. I'm interested in poetry, too. How is it?"   The woman smiled, said goodbye to her friend, and sat back down to begin a conversation with Alan that lasted for some time. A few minutes into their talk, Alan realized that the book had been *her* conversation piece, and that he had almost ignored it!

Chapter 2: Give People Your Card

Suzie had to take the city bus to work after her car broke down, but she hadn't been on a bus in seventeen years. The only reason she even knew where to find the stop was that she'd seen the hordes of London Fog-clad Bostonians sloshing around there on rainy days. When the bus came, she climbed on, but suddenly realized she didn't know how much the fare was. Of course, exact change was required. As she fished for the correct combination of coins (inadvertently stabbing herself with her nail file in the process), she could feel the impatience of the rush-hour crowd rising steadily. After a moment of watching her fruitless search, the bus driver barked, "Lady, put in your change or get off, wouldja?" Then she heard a considerably more friendly voice behind her: "Do you need change?" When she turned in its direction, a man about her age was reaching forward, offering two precious quarters. She thanked him, took the coins gratefully, fed the fare box, and sat down. He sat next to her; they started talking. After a while, just when Suzie was remarking to herself what a great conversationalist her benefactor was, the bus reached her stop.

What should Suzie's next move have been?

One: Thank her new friend and get off the bus.

Two: Stay on the bus rather than avoid breaking off the conversation.

Three: Ask the bus driver if he'd mind waiting a few minutes so the pair could say a civil goodbye.

Four: Reach into her purse (avoiding the nail file this time), hand the change-giver her business card, and ask him to join her for the deli sandwich of his choice as her way of saying thanks.

The correct answer, of course, is the last one. How

many times have you met someone interesting, but found yourself afraid to give them your number or ask for theirs? When circumstances separated you, you probably had no way to get in touch and never saw the person again. Giving out your card solves this problem.

Don't confuse this method with writing your number on a slightly soggy cocktail napkin if you happen to be in a bar when you encounter the person you'd like to see more of. Using napkins as stationery makes it seem obvious that you're looking for a date. Giving someone a business card entails less emotional risk. It's a handy, mature way of saying, "I enjoyed talking with you. Let's do it again." That's all.

The number-on-the-napkin approach has several other serious drawbacks. Napkins may be used, completely innocently, as (guess what?) napkins later on, and you don't want someone sneezing on your contact information. A napkin can also end up in the wash if the receiver forgets about putting it in a pocket. And they have a tendency to tear, smear easily, or become illegible with certain types of pens. Business cards, by contrast, go safely in someone's purse or wallet, and look great.

Giving someone your card (or, conversely, *asking* someone interesting for theirs) is easier and simpler than the napkin routine, as well. Don't make a big deal out of it. Somebody has to take control, and it might as well be you. Make your move confidently and calmly, then smile and keep right on going.

Get in the habit of making the exchange early in the conversation, before the "should-I-get-her-number/when-is-he-going-to-ask-for-my-number" anxiety builds too much. When the person tells you his or her profession, you can just say, "Oh, do you have a card?" Or, to have more control over the situation, you can confidently pass along your card right after you say what *you* do. Either way, you won't come across as someone who's desperate for a date. What's more, you'll be able to enjoy the rest of the conversation without feeling anxious!

Another advantage to handing out business cards is that you don't have to give out your home number unless you want to. If you can't easily take calls at work, don't let that stop you. Just tell the caller who reaches you at your job that you're glad to get the call, but that they've reached you at a bad time. Then ask if you can call them at home that night. (You'll have the advantage of being prepared and a little more relaxed.)

Giving someone your business card is not only a way of making sure they can get in touch with you--it's also a way of establishing credibility. You're someone who has a profession, and who is straightforward about what that profession is.

WHAT IF YOU DON'T HAVE A BUSINESS CARD?

Have some printed!

It's not so unusual. Even if you have a job for which a card doesn't seem appropriate, you may harbor a secret "sideline" ambition that's been on the back burner for a while. If so, a card is a perfect way to make those ideas a little more concrete, and to make a strong personal statement in the process.

Vicki is a waitress, but she designs jewelry part-time at home. Her card reads: "Diamonds in the Rough"!

Tony is a telephone lineman. His business card, however, reflects the fact that he also buys and sells unusual art prints.

Warren, an auto mechanic, collects antique maps as a hobby. Guess which endeavor is highlighted on his business card?

You may be worried that you'll start getting crank calls in the middle of the night if you start handing out your number. That's what Alicia's friends warned her about when she began giving cards to people she met. The fact is, though, that an ad she placed in the paper to sell her sofa bed elicited more nasty calls than she ever received as a result of circulating her card.

Remember to take other people's cards, even if you're involved. The reason? Well, like most of us, you probably find that you'll go for months without a date, then meet three or four great people at the same time. That's not entirely coincidence at work. When you feel confident, charming, and lovable, you project those qualities. They're quite attractive, and people tend to react to them positively. In a way, it's the ultimate cosmic joke--the less attention you need, the more you get.

Shift the odds in your favor by holding on to the cards of intriguing people you meet, even if you're "attached" at the moment. Of course, when you find someone special and things are really clicking, you probably want the romance to last forever. Maybe it will. But that doesn't mean you can't continue to make friends--both men and women. No one's advocating being sleazy here, only that you be open to potential friendships. If things work out well, you may even be able to fix this new friend up with someone else you know. If it turns out you haven't found the love of your life after all . . . what's wrong with being prepared?

Lindsay met Ed in a hospital cafeteria while she was involved in an increasingly unsatisfying live-in relationship. She enjoyed her discussion with Ed and did not want to lose touch with him--but she really wasn't ready to start anything. Yet. So she told Ed she and her boyfriend were thinking about throwing a party, and asked if he'd like to come (noting that a girlfriend of hers who shared Ed's interest in karate would be there, too). She got his card and added his address to the invitation list. Home life grew steadily more rocky; the planned party never materialized. Several months later, after she and her boyfriend broke up, Lindsay sent Ed a little note asking him out for coffee. Not long after that, they started dating.

CHAPTER 3:
Discover How to Make Yourself Feel Desirable

Y ou have to *feel* desirable to *be* desirable. If you're having problems convincing other people that you are indeed a sexy, attractive, stimulating, vibrant being, perhaps the reason is that you haven't yet convinced yourself of this fact. Maybe you think no one worth desiring would desire you.

Nonsense!

Everyone has desirable qualities. Each of us has something unique, something that makes us worthwhile people to know and to love. If you're having trouble believing this, work on it a little harder. Do *not* give up. Make it a habit to remind yourself that you are worthwhile.

How? Identify things you can do that make you feel desirable--*and then do them often!*   The idea is that if you do something that makes you feel great about yourself, you'll end up projecting that desirable image, and you'll be in a better frame of mind to meet new people. You'll get away from your old reliable negative thinking habits, and enter into a more self-confident mode that attracts others.

Where do you start? The following list may give you some ideas.

**ANSWERS WE'VE GOTTEN TO THE QUESTION,
"WHAT MAKES YOU FEEL DESIRABLE?"
(ASKED OF BOTH MEN AND WOMEN)**

Wearing perfume or cologne . . . reading the last two pages of *The Great Gatsby* . . . working out at the gym . . . buying new clothes, even if only a wonderful tie or a colorful silk scarf . . . making a great throw from shortstop to first base . . . taking a sauna . . . singing along with love songs on the radio . . . winking at yourself when you pass a mirror.

Use these suggestions to come up with your own list. When you're thinking about clothes, think about a special outfit you might already have that makes you feel like smiling at strangers or taking more risks. Figure out what it is about these articles that makes you feel so special. Is it the fabric, the color, the fit? Do more of what makes you feel good. Wear more red, spring for a good tailor-made outfit more often if you can, or buy another pair of shoes like the old favorites you finally wore out last year.

Don't wait for a special occasion. Make *today* your special occasion.

Remember: consider things that make you *feel* different on the inside, even if they don't make you *look* any different on the outside.

When Lisa makes up her mind to meet someone special, she has a certain ritual she goes through beforehand. She buys all-new lingerie. Even though she's the only one who knows she's wearing all that silk and lace, the knowledge empowers her. Lisa feels like she's walking around with a great secret, one that makes her feel incredibly sexy and alluring. In this way, she alters her state of mind--a more fundamental change than, say, a token change in her winter wardrobe would be.

Howie goes through a similar ritual. He starts asking good friends over for his exotic "Spaghetti a la Howie," his secret-recipe gourmet specialty. Howie stirs the sauce slowly for hours, tasting it after adding each spice to make sure it has just the right zing. He even sets a lavish table--candles, placecards and all. His dinner parties are such a hit that his guests often ask if they can come back for leftovers! Normally, he doesn't bother with preparing anything that can't be microwaved in less than seven minutes. But when Howie wants to meet his match, he begins pumping himself up by doing something he does really well--something others admire him for.

Don't assume something has to be overtly sexual to make you feel desirable. Sexuality is certainly a part of that sensation, but it isn't the whole story. Desirability is also about confidence. Getting a raise or doing someone a favor can make you feel desirable. So can completing a task you've had on your list of "things to do" for a long time (such as redecorating your living room, or writing to your favorite out-of-state relative, to give two examples). Don't skip ideas like these when your goal is to boost your self-esteem.

Sometimes you don't exactly know what's making you glow. But if you look inward, you'll probably find some concrete reasons that are contributing to this feeling. Concentrate on how to reconstruct the sensation so the experience isn't totally left to chance. You want to be able to recreate the positive, confident, alluring being you've become!

Warning: no one can feel desirable every minute of every day. Not Cher, not Harrison Ford, nobody. Having ups and downs is part of being human. Don't expect yourself to conform to impossible standards.

The best advice is to learn to take advantage of the feeling when you have it . . . and not to castigate yourself endlessly if you feel glum about yourself for a spell. The next time you're feeling desirable, smile at the next person who turns you on--and see what happens!

CHAPTER 4:
Tell People You're Interested in Dating

Has this ever happened to you? You mention to a co-worker or friend that you'd like to meet someone special. The other person is surprised, then says something like, "Oh, come on. You're so sweet (or good-looking, or intelligent, or friendly, or fun to be with) that you shouldn't have any trouble meeting people."

Did your friend, while thinking he or she was paying you a compliment, actually end up dismissing your request? Did the person add a comment like, "Maybe you're too picky," or imply that something was wrong with you because you weren't attached? Did you buy into that drivel and drop the issue?

The truth is, the mere fact of having a lover proves nothing. You're not always happy, and you can't even be sure of being loved. Plenty of wonderful people are in bad relationships with other not-so-wonderful people who mistreat them--or with someone who's simply not right, but to whom they stay attached because of a fear of loneliness. Just because you chose not to subject yourself to such pain or boredom, and are looking now for something a little more stimulating and life-giving, doesn't mean there's anything wrong with you. Whether you have a lover or not says very little about your worth as a *potential* lover.

In other words, if someone looks at you funny because you're alone, that's not your problem. It's your "friend's" problem.

You could just as easily say in response, "Why are you with that slimy jerk who calls you 'Main Squeeze'?" But you don't. You have compassion, manners, and a sense of tact. You know better. Real friends should have the same attitude toward you.

In this chapter, we'll learn why taking the chance of telling people you're interested in dating could well be worth any odd responses you might get.

WHAT YOU MIGHT SAY

> *You:* (Looking your friend George straight in the eye during a casual conversation.) George, I've decided to start dating. If you meet someone or know someone interesting who's available, could you keep me in mind?

(Alternate approach--"Laugh and the World Laughs With You":)

> *You:* George, I'd like to start dating someone really interesting. If you meet someone who speaks Lithuanian and plays the harmonica, keep me in mind, okay?

(Second alternate approach--"An Abundance of Riches":)

> *You:* George, I've been going out a lot lately--you know, looking for the right person--and I'd like to meet even more new women. If you think of anyone you know I might hit it off with, will you keep me in mind?

WHAT MIGHT HAPPEN WHEN YOU TRY IT

> *George:* Sure. (Conversation continues normally, and moves on to other topics.)

(Or, if George is not quite up to speed on tact:)

> *George:* You? What's the matter? Don't tell me you're having trouble getting dates--

> *You:* Thanks. I appreciate it. Hey, wasn't today your deadline for that huge project you've been working on all month? How'd it go? (Conversation continues normally.)

THE FOLLOW-UP

> *You:* (At the end of your visit with George, as you are preparing to part company.) Remember about my little favor, all right? There's a night on the town out

there with my name on it.

The objective is to state your intention clearly and simply without belaboring the point. Then, after time has passed, remind the person of your request (especially if you're in a confident mood). After all, your social life is not the number-one priority for this person. The reminder also reinforces the fact that your request for help was a serious one.

Melanie once asked a colleague, Jane, if she knew anyone Melanie might like to meet. Jane's response: "Gee, you're such a nice person. I can't believe you have trouble meeting men." Melanie smiled and assured Jane she was indeed available, then changed the subject. A month or so passed, and one afternoon, Melanie tried again with humor and tact. Jane, busy working on a report, thought for a moment, but said she didn't know anyone Melanie would be interested in. A few weeks later, Melanie gave a gentle reminder over lunch. Suddenly Jane snapped her fingers and said, "You know, I *do* know a fellow who lives in the apartment across the hall from me who told me he'd like to meet someone nice. I'll give him your number."

Keith spent a lot of time moping around after his wife left him. His mother, Norma, wanted to help, but Keith was sure there was nothing she could do. How many young woman friends could she have? On the train home from a bad day at work, Norma sat next to Debbie, who was recovering from her own bad day. Norma and Debbie really hit it off, and Norma sensed that Debbie and Keith might like each other. She invited Debbie to stop by after dinner for a liqueur--but didn't "hype" her son to her new friend. That evening, Keith came for dinner, and Norma mentioned that a new friend she'd met on the train was stopping by. After the meal, the doorbell rang. The rest of the evening went quite well, and Debbie and Keith started going out together shortly thereafter.

As the last anecdote suggests, you shouldn't forget to

include relatives on your list of folks to ask. Even your parents, whom you may consider unlikely candidates for this sort of networking, have probably met quite a few friends since you left home. New friends their age probably have children/nieces/nephews/neighbors who are around *your* age. Remember that most parents will expend a lot of energy to make their children happy. If you take advantage of that energy, something interesting may come your way. Don't laugh--it happens!

YOUR CONTACT PUTS YOU IN TOUCH WITH SOMEONE: NOW WHAT?

Remember George? Well, he took your friendly request seriously, and he's just called to say he knows someone you might want to meet. What do you do?

First, stay calm. Ask about the mystery man/woman, but don't overwhelm your intermediary. Specifically, don't ask if the person is ready for a relationship. George, in all likelihood, does not know the answer to this question. And even if the person in question doesn't think he or she is ready, that may be because he or she hasn't met *you* yet. Right?

Try to set up a way of meeting this person that *de-emphasizes the dating aspect.* Maybe George could throw a pot luck dinner and invite you both. Or maybe the other person works in the kind of setting that would allow you and George to drop by for a minute.

If these ideas won't work, call the person and say you'll be in the neighborhood on such-and-such a day. Ask if you can get together for coffee. Make the first encounter brief. Don't spend your first meeting discussing ex-significant others. (They've since become *insignificant* others, as far as you two are concerned.)

If you adore each other, you can make plans. If not, meeting for a quick cup of coffee allows you to have a brief conversation, make a new friend, and part company gracefully without wasting time, money, or emotional energy.

CHAPTER 5:
Learn to
Type Shift

Type shifting has nothing to do with capital letters on a keyboard. It has to do with broadening your mind. Let's try a simple test. Do you agree with the following statement?

"It would surprise me if someone with the color hair that I never preferred, or the body type that doesn't do much for me, or even an occupation I considered dull, turned out to be better suited to me than the people I *think* are my type--the people who keep letting me down."

If you disagreed, good for you. If you agreed, then your objective is to date a *type* (a list of attributes) rather than a *person* (a living, breathing entity).

A type is what you scan the bar or party for. A person is the unique mind, warm body, and captivating spirit you have a relationship with.

THE ADVANTAGES
OF STAYING FLEXIBLE

People who are flexible in establishing who they're willing to go out with have more options than people who aren't. Don't panic; we're not talking about lowering your standards, or "settling" for someone in whom you have no genuine interest. "Settling" is hopping on a wagon train bound for California in 1860. Type shifting is taking a closer look at yourself, as well as other people, and learning what truly matters to you.

After all, wouldn't you be offended if you overheard someone you were attracted to say you weren't their type? You'd probably think the person was shallow for sizing you up too quickly and stereotyping you. And you'd be right.

When you dismiss someone out of hand as being "not your type," you're not looking at all of the person's attributes, and you're ignoring what makes each person you meet unique.

If your type is *"Italian Stallion"* . . . don't overlook a guy who doesn't know linguine from lug wrenches, but who serenades you on summer evenings and can't stop sending you roses.

If your type is *"Sun Worshipper"* . . . don't overlook a woman who refuses to sunbathe because she finds it boring, but who can't get enough scuba diving, sailing, and windsurfing.

If your type is *"Literary Lion"* . . . don't overlook someone who didn't graduate from the Ivies, but who took a night job to pay for community college classes in English Literature, a lifelong passion.

James learned about typeshifting when he met a woman at work, Betty, whom he liked very much, but didn't think was his type. As the days passed, however, and as he got to know her better and better, he realized that he might have been a little extreme in his first judgment. Then it happened. One day, during their coffee break, James learned of Betty's interest in opera--one of his lifelong loves. This certainly wasn't the sort of thing he expected to hear from her! Then again, he wouldn't have expected to hear her accept, with a gleam in her eye, his invitation to see a performance of *Madame Butterfly!*

Two of Eleanor's significant relationships over the past few years were with men she knew for at least a full year before she even remotely considered them as possible dating material. The first man, Donald, was living with someone when she met him. She thought he was brash, cocky, and not her type at all. But Eleanor and Donald built up a fine friendship. Once Donald's live-in relationship ended, Eleanor realized that she was actually attracted to Donald-- but that she would never have felt that anything could happen between them if they had not first built their "neutral" friendship.

Mindy is a pianist whose first date with Jeffrey, a sailor, was a disaster. Jeffrey kept talking about his dream of living on a ship with an Oriental wife and three kids, which left Mindy feeling seasick. She considered Jeffrey a complete waste of time, but he liked her and kept calling over the next few weeks. She began to refer to him as "the thing that wouldn't go away"--but for some reason she kept agreeing to see him! Eventually, something strange happened. Jeffrey decided to go to law school so he could specialize in maritime law. He settled down, stopped talking about living on a boat, and, about eight months after their first date, asked Mindy to marry him. She did. Although they're quite happy together, Mindy still laughs about Jeffrey not being her type.

Start with people you already know or know of. Sit down and make a list of all the available but previously overlooked possible partners in your circle of friends. (Of course, you should not include people you've already dated.)

Be sure to list the unlikely candidates: your neighbor who cheerfully signs for packages when you're out of town; your best friend's cousin, who's into palmistry, and whom you always wrote off as a bit eccentric; the person your mother thinks you should see but who can't possibly be right for you because your mother is never right about these things.

Is there anyone on your list you haven't really thought about in "that way," but whom you might just be able to think about in "that way" if you stopped to think about it?

TYPE SHIFTING YOURSELF

You should also consider being flexible about the kind of person you think you are.

If you're convinced you'd hate square dancing, give it a try. Maybe you did hate it in your third grade gym class, but perhaps now--with the right people--you might get quite a kick out of it. Do you consider yourself the sort who'd never wear a mini-skirt? Or read the personals section of a newspaper? Or invite a bunch of people to your place for dinner? Don't sell yourself short--and never say never.

Type shifting occurs when you begin to develop a new, more open attitude toward the people you meet. Type shifting allows you to give up daydreaming and take a realistic look at who is actually walking through the door.

This doesn't mean you'll end up dating all the people who return a smile, but you might just surprise yourself when you see how your "base" of interesting prospects begins to grow.

CHAPTER 6:
Identify Where You
Get Stuck
Most Often

Everyone gets stuck somewhere. Maybe you're fine talking to power dressers who remind you of your baby brother (now a high-level executive), but your tongue turns to stone with any man who seems more at home in flannel shirts than French cuffs. If so, initiating conversation is probably a sticking point for you.

This is a common obstacle--and one that's so important that it will be treated extensively a little later in this book-- but it's not the *only* place people get stuck.

Many of us get stuck well before we even think about saying hello because our fears get in the way. These fears are typically camouflaged with sweeping generalizations. Don't be fooled, either by these pseudo-truths or those touting them (including yourself).

BE WARY WHEN YOU HEAR . . .

"Women today are just too aggressive."

"Men today still aren't sensitive enough."

"All the *good* men are taken."

"All the *good* women are taken."

"No one will be willing to give me the space I need."

"No one will be willing to make a real commitment."

"All the women I meet just want someone who can spend a lot of money on them."

"All the men I meet think all they have to do is spend a lot of money for me to be impressed."

Statements like these merely enable you to avoid pinpointing, facing, and resolving your own issues. Placing the responsibility on something "out there" will not solve your problem, but only compound it.

A seminar participant of ours once complained that she couldn't possibly find a man, because there were 30,000 single women in her city, compared with 10,000 single men. "You mean," came the response, "that there are 10,000 men out there, and all you have to do is find one you could love? Those are *great* odds!" The moral of the story is that just about everything depends on how you look at your situation. If you give statistics (or anything beyond your control) more power than you give yourself, you're asking for trouble.

Another common sticking point: perhaps you have a "dark secret" you're afraid someone will discover. If so, you might consider dropping you guard a bit. Now, no one's suggesting that you broadcast *real* secrets, like the fact that you had your name legally changed from "Fuzzy," or that you're wanted by Interpol. The issue here is the secret you have no logical reason for concealing--the secret that only perpetuates your own negative cycles. Consider these:

SILLY SECRETS

"If I talk to this person, he or she will discover how boring I really am, and will never want to go out with me."

"If I talk to this man, he will think I want to go out with him--and if he's married or living with someone (which he probably is) I'll make a complete fool of myself. If he's not attached, he probably doesn't want to go out with someone like me anyway, so I'll *still* make a complete fool of myself."

"If I ask this woman out on a date, she'll want to know more about me before she decides. Once she learns what kind of guy I am, the answer will be no. None of the worthwhile women ever want to date me."

"If I try to engage in a conversation with this person, he (she) will probably realize I'm not his (her) type, and come up with some excuse for walking away--like remembering an important call he (she) has to make."

All of these "secret fears" are, of course, completely imaginary. But imagination is often so powerful that it allows you to determine the outcome before the event. What you imagine to be true comes true not because it represents anything fundamental about you--but because you make it true.

Remember, the anxiety you feel in an encounter doesn't necessarily come from what's actually happening, but is much more likely to originate from your own wild, unceasing, occasionally uncompassionate, all-too-often-off-the-mark imagination. You wouldn't put up with treatment like that from somebody else, so don't put up with such nonsense from yourself. Take a reality check instead.

THE REALITY BEHIND THE SILLY SECRETS

"If I talk to this person, he or she may find me boring--but probably not, since I can be quite engaging when I wish to be."

"If I talk to this man, he may think I want to go out with him--and he may want to go out with me, too. If the guy is already attached, he'll probably be flattered. And you never know, he might have an unattached brother, or roommate, or cousin, or . . . "

"If I ask this woman out and the answer is no, there's no reason for me to take it personally. Maybe she's already attached--or in a lousy mood. But if she says yes, I'm sure we'll have a great time."

"If this person doesn't consider me 'the right type,' it doesn't mean I'm not anyone else's type. I can't expect to be entertaining to everyone I meet, and I certainly don't expect everyone I meet to entertain me. Anyway, I'll never know unless I try!"

George went to a singles dance with high expectations. He asked a woman to dance and she turned him down cold. He felt marked after that--as if every other woman knew he'd been rejected once, and, therefore, considered him less appealing. Later that evening, George concluded that what had really happened was that his imagination had taken control. He decided that next time, he'd meet his enemy head-on. He worked up a little speech: "Hello, imagination. Did you know you're manipulative, misleading, and addicted to failure? Did you know I feel absolutely great tonight? Did you know that there are many women who've enjoyed dancing with me before, and that if the next one doesn't want to, it's her loss, not mine? Did you know that someone turning me down only results in more time for the women who *do* want to trip the light fantastic with an extraordinarily attractive, suave man like yours truly?"

Sometimes people get stuck because they have Hidden Agendas. On the outside, there's an open, attractive person who's carefree and pleasant--but underneath, there's a hall monitor with a clipboard and a whistle around the neck, checking off items on a list. Typically, the first item on that list is: "Is this one marriageable material?"

Of course, it's normal for two single people to have that topic on their minds (consciously or unconsciously) to some degree. But the single who gets stuck in the Hidden Agenda usually makes the "marriage meter" the single most noticeable aspect of his or her character.

These are the people who ask pointed questions about a date's job, address, previous spouses and/or lovers, substance abuse, whether or not the person likes kids, has kids already, or might be interested in having *their* kids. And that's just in the first ten minutes.

If you think you might fall into this category, don't be too hard on yourself. Stop and think about how you would feel if you were subjected to this kind of cross-examination at the very beginning of a relationship. You'd probably feel as though you were being probed--and you probably wouldn't bother to see whether the person had any other interesting qualities than a ferocious desire to get married.

People will reveal themselves to you at their own rate, no matter what you do or how many questions you ask. You can help them along, but if you push too hard and/or too early, you'll drive them away. The pressure of being "grilled," of being expected to provide the "right" answers or risk seeing the relationship aborted, of watching yourself be reduced to a series of responses on a checklist, is intense and unpleasant.

The person with the Hidden Agenda is usually concerned about wasting time. Who wants to spend four years with someone who's obviously not Mr. or Ms. Right?

Nevertheless, while you may feel that spending four years with the "wrong" person is a waste of time (an arguable point, since you're likely to learn *something* in that period), years are simply not the scale you're working in at the outset of a relationship. Three or four dates with someone is a more realistic framework to consider, and such an interval really shouldn't be considered a waste of time if things don't work out.

If you've spent the last four years of your life with The

Wrong Person, is it really fair to hold that against someone you've spoken to for ten minutes? Is it their fault you stayed in a losing relationship? There is no way around it. You will have to build a little trust before you can learn anything substantial about your potential partner. Give yourself time.

CHAPTER 7:
Give Someone
A Second Chance

Michelle, who considered herself something of a matchmaker, thought that Flo, a music lover, would be perfect for Tom, an attractive and talented musician. She gave Tom Flo's number, and shortly thereafter the two made plans to meet. A few days later, Michelle got a call from Flo. "Why did you bother?" Flo asked. "He seems nice enough, but he was so quiet; he hardly said a word all evening. He's Mr. Dull." This was not the Tom Michelle knew--in her experience, Tom was witty, alive, charming, a great conversationalist, and anything but dull. Michelle urged Flo to give Tom another chance, which, with some hesitation, she did. Several weeks later, Michelle got another call from Flo. This time, it was to say thanks. She had fallen in love with Mr. Dull, who had become quite interesting when given the opportunity.

Sometimes, when two people meet for the first time (especially when they meet on a blind date with high expectations) they get overanxious with the whole damn business and clam up.

The person may look like he or she is not trying to initiate conversation, not trying to get to know you. You may think your partner is dull and uninteresting because he or she won't look you in the eye, or because they give every indication of not having a good time. You may even think that the worst has happened, and that The Terrible Truth About You has finally come to light, that this person has discovered at last that *you* are a dull, uninteresting, unexciting, and/or unattractive person.

Give yourself a break. And give your date one while you're at it.

Sometimes people who are personable and fun to be

with will "put up a front." That's a natural enough reaction, especially if you're nervous about meeting someone or feeling vulnerable. Unfortunately, this can happen even if you're wonderful and easy to talk to and give every sign of being the perfect lifelong partner. Even if all that is coming across beautifully, the person doesn't really know you yet.

There's another category of people who deserve a second chance: those who try too hard. These are the people who seem annoying at first, the ones you're tempted to write off early. In reality, though, they're not offensive or arrogant--just nervous, with an unfortunate way of showing it.

SIGNS OF TRYING TOO HARD
Talking too much and/or too loudly
Laughing excessively
Making lots of compliments
Drinking and/or smoking excessively

People who try too hard also have a tendency to: tell you the history of their old lovers just to save you the time if you have any of the same qualities; shred napkins or make strange sculptures out of drink straws; tip over their water glass while reaching for the guacamole; tip over your water glass while trying to wipe up the water from their tipped-over water glass.

Fortunately, none of this necessarily represents a lifelong addiction to boorish behavior.

KEEP AN OPEN MIND
Don't automatically assume that someone you've just met is really dull. Or obnoxious. Or uninterested in you. Such dates may simply be nervous. Give them a second chance. Allow a little more time to pass before your first impressions become final verdicts.

Granted, sometimes blind dates do turn out to be totally wrong for you, uncoordinated or dull or offensive even when they're not nervous. How can you tell the gems from the jerks? Use the following list as a rough guideline.

SIGNS OF NOT TRYING AT ALL

Not being able to keep his eyes off the woman with the large breasts at the next table.

Repeatedly going out to the car to check on the dog that wasn't allowed in the restaurant, but that couldn't be left at home for fear of hurting the pet's feelings.

Getting up from dinner to make a date for after-dinner drinks with someone else.

Snoring over salad.

Wearing a Sony Walkman during dinner.

Asking if you mind if she balances the checkbook over dinner.

Spending the whole date talking about how lousy her ex was in bed, and passing along her pet name for the ex's genitals.

WHEN TO GIVE A SECOND CHANCE

The key, of course, is to learn to tell the difference between those who *look* like they're not trying, or *look* like they're trying too hard, and those who are not trying at all. There is a difference, and if you look closely enough, you should be able to pick up on it.

Life would indeed be wonderful if all of us could immediately connect like Romeo and Juliet, or engage in the facile repartee of Beatrice and Benedick, complete with passionate verbal conflicts whose sole purpose is to cover a deep, abiding attraction.

If only it were so. If only there were never awkward pauses or empty glances into space. If only we were at our best each moment, forever on the money, eternally confident and in control each moment of our effortless, smoothly flowing lives.

It usually doesn't work out that way, of course. Some people need more time to blossom than others. Haven't you ever said of an acquaintance, "You've really got to wait until you get to know her; she takes a little time to warm up to, but she's wonderful."

And don't you think the same thing could be true of you? *You* know you're pretty terrific, but does everyone you meet figure this out within the first five minutes? Think back for a moment. Have *you* always come across as confident, attractive, and unflappable in dealing with others?

Wasn't there ever a time when you felt you'd blown an

opportunity because of something you did or said that you thought was really dumb?

(Cringe here.)

Don't you wish *you* had gotten a second chance?

CHAPTER 8:
Make a
Wish/Need List

Herb spent twelve years learning to play bridge. He plays four nights a week. He'd love to have a wife who plays bridge so they could share that part of his life, but he's a lousy teacher and he knows it. Herb's made up his mind. He's not interested in any woman who doesn't play bridge. He wants a partner at his level now--not in three years.

Sound vaguely familiar? Lots of people insist that potential mates meet specific criteria before even being considered. Anything less represents a compromise, and compromise is not what these people are about.

The problem is that the Herbs of this world miss out on the Natalies. Natalie is a tall, intelligent, redhead with a real love for life--who doesn't play bridge. She does play tennis, though, and would love to meet a man with his own interests so she could continue playing tennis several nights a week.

No, the Herbs of this world tend to end up with Julias. Julia plays bridge, all right. She eats, thinks, and sleeps bridge, as a matter of fact. The funny thing is, every time Herb takes her out, he feels she's more interested in bridge than she is in him! Of course, he loves playing as her partner, but he wants more. And he can't seem to get it. She never looks longingly in his eyes . . . never asks about what happened to him during the day . . . never seems interested in Herb outside of bridge games. Last week, when he was telling her about a fierce migraine headache he had, she changed the subject abruptly and began to question him about a bid he'd made the night before. She considered it shaky at best, she said.

Herb still thinks he needs someone who plays bridge, but he's decided he also needs someone who cares about his feelings. What he needs most of all is to think about the difference between what he really needs and what he'd like very much to have.

Perhaps you're like Herb in some ways. Maybe you're looking for a mate who can share your passions for skiing, sailing, jogging, dancing, or dieting. Maybe you love all those endeavors and want someone who shares your enthusiasm for each of them. You could join every club in a 50-mile radius that caters to each hobby, and then scan the lists to find someone who, like you, joined each one. But you probably wouldn't find someone who shared all those interests. Fortunately, you don't need to.

"YOU CAN'T ALWAYS GET WHAT YOU WANT . . ."

You *can* have what you really need and *some* of what you really want, but not until you identify what these things are. So go sit in a quiet room where you won't be disturbed, take out a pencil and paper, and draw a line down the middle. On one side, write "Wish List," and on the other, "Need List." Then start writing. Here's how it might look.

WISH LIST
I wish he could dance.
I wish he loved *film noir.*
I wish he had wavy, blond hair.
I wish he were 6' 1".

NEED LIST
He's got to let me dance.
I need him to be able to make a commitment to me if the relationship becomes serious.
He has to listen to me when I'm concerned about something.
He has to be able to make me laugh.

As you compose your list, think about your past loves--what they provided you with, and, just as important, what was missing. Be sure to give special considerations to the ones that really claimed a chunk of your heart. How did each stack up against your wish/need list? Have you ever had a lover who provided every single item on the wish list, but didn't do so well on the need list? Did you spend a lot of time wondering why things weren't gelling--why this person was "everything you wanted" but still not enough? Now do you know why?

Your list may have to be amended from time to time, perhaps even from date to date at the outset. Nothing should be chiseled in stone; by the same token, you shouldn't be afraid to write a wish or need down, even if the list would look a little funny to someone else. If in doubt, write it down--you'll get better and better at focusing in on what is really important to you.

Now let's go back to Herb. Is it possible he is insisting that his next lover play bridge because his ex, Danielle, tried to get him to give up his hobby? Is it possible Herb is confusing having a respect for his need to play with having the ability to play at his level?

Tony was talking to a female psychologist at a party. "I'm 53 now," he said. "I think I'm finally ready to get married." "Is that so?" the psychologist asked. "What sort of woman are you looking for?" "Well," Tony replied, "I'm short, so she should be under 5' 4", and I love to jog, so she should jog, too. I also love jazz; she really ought to share my taste in music. I couldn't bear having to listen to Led Zeppelin or anything like that. And I'm a diabetic; it would be good if she were into natural foods. Oh, yes, she can't smoke, either. I hate the smell of cigarette smoke." The psychologist looked at him and smiled. "You know, Tony," she said, "I don't think you're looking for a wife at all. I think you're looking for a mirror image of yourself, someone to point to at dinner parties and show your friends to prove what a great idea *you* were."

Wishes are preferences. Needs are essential. Wishes go on the top of the pyramid, but the pyramid can't be built without a solid foundation. Find out what that foundation is, and then build on it.

CHAPTER 9:
Don't Take Yourself
Too Seriously

Building your social life, meeting new people, and finding a lover are all supposed to be fun. If you aren't having any fun with these activities, you owe it to yourself to find out why, and to make a change for the better.

This is not to say that something is wrong if you occasionally get the blues. You are human, after all, and people have bad days from time to time. What's more, following the advice in this book often entails taking some risks, and sometimes risks don't work out as well as we might hope.

What you should watch out for, though, is constant worrying and self-deprecation. If you find yourself placed under constant cross-examination by a little voice in the back of your head, watch out. There's no need for anguish and self-doubt on such issues as whether or not you're "doing it right," or whether you should try the book's suggestions in a different order, or whether you should start all over again from the top after you have plastic surgery. Go easy on yourself.

If you are not having much fun because you worry too much about what you're doing, how you're doing it, and whether or not it's doing any good, chances are you're taking yourself too seriously. Perhaps you think it's not that big a problem. Perhaps you think you take yourself as seriously as necessary, and it suits you fine. If so, please take a few minutes out for this simple test.

**THE "JUST HOW SERIOUSLY IS
TOO SERIOUSLY?" TEST**

(For each item, note whether
you agree or disagree.)

I can't stand my laugh; it sounds so undignified. *Agree/Disagree*

I don't go to beach parties because I don't like the way I look in a bathing suit. *Agree/Disagree*

I would never ask someone out unless I had a pretty good idea that I could marry him/her. *Agree/Disagree*

I don't like to make last-minute changes in plans or spur-of-the-moment arrangements because I strive for discipline and order in my life. *Agree/Disagree*

If I won $500,000 in the lottery, I'd pay off all my loans and credit cards, open an IRA, make a few charitable contributions, and then put every penny left over into a savings fund so that my as-yet-unborn children would be able to go to college. *Agree/Disagree*

With every "agree" you even remotely considered checking, you entered further into the I-Take-Myself-Too-Seriously Zone. The following statements should be ones with which high scorers are either familiar or identify with.

"I'm a 38-year old woman who wants a family. I don't have any time to waste."

"The last woman I dated put my ego through the Cuisinart, so the next time I'm going to be very careful about who I ask out."

"I have two jobs and no spare time to worry about preliminaries. Either I click with someone immediately, or I forget about 'em."

These statements, and the dozens more just like them you may hear these days, contain generous helpings of both hostility and desperation. Maybe you have good reasons for being desperate or hostile; many people do. But think for a minute.

Think back to a time when you were involved with someone and feeling so damn good about yourself that you would have had no problem connecting with any number of different people--people with whom, under other circumstances, you could have had a non-platonic relationship. Virtually everyone has experienced this. Did you ever wonder why? It's because when you project satisfaction with yourself, other people find that a big turn-on. Conversations with you are pleasant. Your pace was relaxed and open. You were confident, centered, and approachable.

On the other hand, when you project desperation or hostility, you're not much fun to be around. You don't usually let things develop at their natural pace. You scare people off--*even people who also want a family or who have sworn never to put someone's ego through the Cuisinart.*

Fortunately, you have a choice. You don't have to be desperate or hostile. You *can* work your way back to that confident, relaxed you that was so attractive. Honest.

Albert asked Laura, a woman in her late thirties, out to dinner. He had been very interested in her, but when they reached the restaurant, before the waiter had so much as poured the water, she let loose with this speech: "Look. I'm thirty-seven. I want a family. I don't have time to play around. If you aren't interested in the same goals, we should quit right here."   Albert sat silently, stunned. As it turned out, he did share her goals. But he certainly didn't share Laura's attitude, and he concluded that he did not want to pursue those goals with her.

Part of the "trick" of connecting with someone is to appear as though you're *not* feverishly searching for the relationship of your life. Sure--if the real thing comes along, you're open to it. But *you are not an incomplete person if you don't find it by next Wednesday.*

Feeling desperate carries even more disadvantages, the most obvious of which is that you're likely to attract the dreaded Exploiters of Desperation. You might not spot them at first; your perceptions aren't always clear when you're desperate. But they're out there, waiting for innocent victims to look longingly into their eyes. Don't let yourself fall prey to users and abusers.

KEEPING YOUR CHIN UP

Another reason people take themselves too seriously is that they think they're the only ones in the world going through what they're going through--that no one else encounters the difficulties they are having with single life.

Fact: there are 65 million single adults out there today, a figure that remains accurate even if it seems that all your friends are engaged or happily married.

Feeling alone in your situation and actually *being* alone in it are two different things. Don't condemn your environment. Stay objective. Stay open to possibilities. Stay positive!

Finally, remember that finding humor in a situation helps you avoid taking things too seriously; a healthy sense of humor reflects (and strengthens) a certain confidence. Think about someone you know who can laugh at the bad things in life as well as the good. Now think of someone who's panicked all the time. Which person is more fun to be around?   Which person do you consider more attractive?

CHAPTER 10:
Practice
Initiating
Conversation

I nitiating conversation can be terrifying, especially when the person you want to speak to is attractive. It gets even worse if this attractive person actually shows signs of interest in you.

It's one of those cruel paradoxes: the more likely an initial conversation is to lead to something interesting, the more likely we are to freeze.

Jeanne is an attractive woman with a real gift for conversation. She has an engaging smile that she beams readily at just about everyone. She meets men frequently during her commute, in the supermarket, in her office building--just about everywhere. She finds herself chatting amiably to many of these men. But the moment one shows interest in her or asks to see her again, Jeanne becomes utterly tongue-tied, and botches many opportunities.

All beginnings--registration at school, the first day of a job, a move to a strange new city--carry with them a certain degree of "built-in" anxiety. Feeling fear in these situations is normal; after all, you're engaged in something important with people you don't yet know.

Feeling a few butterflies in your stomach, however, doesn't stop you from going to school, or taking a great new job, or moving to another city that offers you a better lifestyle. That same feeling shouldn't stand in your way when it comes to talking to interesting new people, either. Fortunately, it doesn't have to.

CONQUERING "COLD FEET"

Many people avoid initiating conversations because they think of people they don't yet know as strangers--a group we often consider intimidating. If this is a problem for you, try reminding yourself that new people are only strangers until you meet them. After all, every single one of the good friends you have today were strangers to you one.

The best way to get over a fear of initiating conversation is to practice. Say hello to lots and lots of people--every day. Practice on the postman, the clerk at the convenience store, the people in your building . . . in short, anyone. You may want to begin by practicing on people you encounter casually during the course of the day, but can't see yourself dating.

If you make saying hello automatic, you'll keep saying hello from being traumatic. By the time it's second nature for you to issue a sincere, friendly greeting to people, it will be easier to utter the same greeting to someone attractive. Certainly you won't be singling the person out. You say hello to everyone! You are friendly, and you make it a habit to issue a relaxed, pleasant hello to the people you encounter. Right?

Remember that the beginnings of conversations with new people are where you want to use your conversation piece. If you don't have a conversation piece with you, you'll have to create one. The best way to do this is by asking a question of some sort--one that doesn't have a yes-or-no answer.

Why? People who might really like to talk with you might also be shy. Many will want to talk, but will need some help and direction. If you ask a question they can answer with a yes-or-no response, they might not be able to think of what to say next after they answer. Because you're getting good at this sort of thing, you can help them out.

HOW IT MIGHT SOUND

Suppose you're waiting in line to see a movie, and you notice an attractive woman waiting, too. You walk up to her, smile, and start this conversation:

> *You:*   Hi. I was noticing your scarf. I really like that look. My sister's birthday is next week, and I think she would really love something like that. Could you tell me where you got it?

She: Bloomingdales.

You: Great. Hmm. The only problem is that her winter coat is purple. Do you think that scarf would go with a purple coat? Or does it come in different colors?

Then, with any luck, you'll enter into a discussion of women's scarves, after which you can ask her about the movie, discuss how you saw the star in another film in which he was terribly miscast, and so on.

If she keeps talking to you, she is enjoying the conversation. If she excuses herself to go to the ladies' room, then comes out and talks to you again, then she's enjoying the conversation but she had to use the john. If she excuses herself and goes into the ladies room and doesn't come back out, enjoy the movie.

Maybe movies aren't your problem. Maybe you have more difficulty at a social event like a party, where people are "expected" to mingle and start conversations. You realize that you don't have the element of surprise working in your favor here, and before too long you notice that the hostess is running out of paper napkins for you to twist.

If you see someone you'd like to meet, but don't know how to start talking to the person, try this. Walk over and say, "Hi. I'm looking for my friend Wanetta. Do you know her? We promised to meet here under the Gaugin [next to the philodendron] [under the wall clock] and I don't see her. I guess I'll just wait here a few minutes." If no sparks appear after you chat for a few minutes, you can leave.

(Warning: if your new friend asks what Wanetta looks like, you should be able to answer him.)

Here's another approach. If you're near the buffet, you can use the food as a conversation piece. It might sound like this: "Have you tried the egg rolls? They're great, but watch out for the mustard." This technique works equally well for a wide variety of menu items, including rolled-up tubes of bologna with colored toothpicks stuck through them.

Don't limit yourself to starting conversation at parties, movies, or similar settings where people are just standing around. Be inventive.

David, who works in a large office building, had been meaning to return a glove his sister had left in his car. One day after work, he got an idea. As everyone was making for the cars in the parking lot, he kept his eyes open for a woman who appealed to him. Once he did, he grabbed the glove and went over to her. "Excuse me," he said. "I found this in the lot near your car. Is it yours?" Then he gave her his card and asked her to show the glove around her office and return it to him if she had no luck. That way he got to see her again, even though they didn't strike up a conversation the first time!

Hallway hellos can be another tough situation for the aspiring conversation-starter. There's an interesting-looking person who hasn't been introduced to you, but whom you smile at every time you pass in the hall (or elevator, or cafeteria, or weight room). How do you get beyond this stage?

With a little effort and some advance planning, you can ease past this obstacle in a particularly intriguing manner--*if* you can at least find out the person's name. (Fortunately, this is not difficult in most work settings.)

Step One. You find out the man's name is Orville. The next time you see him, say "Hello, Orville." Then go about your business. Orville is going to wonder how you found out his name, which is exactly what you want.

Step Two. Find out something else about Orville. Maybe he just moved to your area from San Francisco. The next time you see him, say, "Hey, someone told me you just moved here from San Francisco. I've been thinking about going out there for a visit next month. Do you know any great restaurants I shouldn't miss?" Or maybe he sails. Say, "I heard you sail. I've been planning to take lessons this summer. Do you know a good place to learn?"

If the above seems impractical because you can't get any more information about the person than a name, here's the next best option. Try asking for an opinion: "I just switched hairdressers, and I think this one cut my hair too short. What do you think?"

Most people like being asked for their opinion. (Think of how many people *volunteer* an opinion without being asked.)   If the Gallup Poll people can do it, so can you. And aren't you much more interesting to talk to than some faceless canvasser working door to door, clutching a pen and clipboard?

CHAPTER 11:
Establish Credibility Early

Signals sometimes get crossed at the outset of a conversation. While this is inevitable, you can shift the odds in your favor, and experience fewer "bail-outs," if you establish your own credibility early on in the conversation.

It must have been the hundredth time it had happened to her, Michelle thought to herself the next morning as she was getting ready to go to work. She'd met a man at the refreshment counter during the intermission of a play she'd gone to see. They ended up talking for fifteen minutes; he seemed pretty friendly, but the whole time he never really told her anything about himself. She kept wondering, "What is a nice guy like this doing here alone?" She expected a date to materialize any minute; when one didn't, the possibility that she'd encountered some sort of psychopath crossed her mind. Finally, he shifted the coat he'd been holding, and she saw the wedding ring on his hand. He said he'd enjoyed talking to her, then informed her that he had to go. He disappeared into the crowd. It infuriated Michelle when she thought of how much time she spent working her hopes up about men who turned out to be married.

James spent twenty minutes before his aerobics class flirting with a woman in a Star Trek sweatshirt who was clearly flirting back. The connection seemed to be strengthening during the workout session. After class, he asked for her number; she told him she was married. "Why on earth," he wondered later, "did she waste my time? A whole aerobics class full of single women, and all I have to show for it is a set of sore muscles!"

Michelle, James, and thousands of others who've had similar experiences might have benefited from a little sign hung around the neck that read:

I AM NOT MARRIED.

I AM NOT A MANIAC.

I HAVE NO DESIRE TO LEAD
YOU ON FOR THE HECK OF IT.

I AM CURIOUS TO LEARN
WHETHER THE SAME
COULD BE SAID ABOUT YOU.

Obviously, you have to be a bit cleverer than that. How can you assure someone you're for real, available, and approachable? How can you keep your own cruises down "blind alleys" to a minimum, while still remaining the subtle, tactful, mature individual you are?

A FEW WAYS TO ESTABLISH CREDIBILITY EARLY

Here are some suggestions on tackling the problems that can present themselves during the "sizing each other up" stage.

Offer your name first. Don't wait for the other person to initiate the introduction. That shows you're not afraid to give out information about yourself.

Offer your business card if you want the other person to have your phone number. Besides telling the person how to reach you, a business card anchors you in the real world. Giving one out also means you're not afraid of people knowing more about you than your name and hair color.

If you ask for the other person's number, ask for the work number. Then suggest that you get together for lunch or coffee. Your counterpart will feel less threatened, since you'll be making it clear that your intention is something other than calling up in the middle of the night to make an obscene phone call. Less risk equals greater likelihood of later contact.

Find a way to let the person know you're single. This is not the same thing as asking whether your counterpart is single, nor is it the same as being blatant about your status by saying something like, "You know, I don't think I've had a real date since the Carter Administration," then laughing nervously. You can set the stage by making some comment about eating a lot of frozen dinners, or belonging to a singles group, or living alone. *Don't set yourself up to sound like a loser.* Offer information about yourself, but don't whine about your divorce or your last breakup in an effort to prove you're unattached. The other person will not only be bored, but will also wonder what it is about you that caused the last relationship to fail.

Women: watch your ring finger. Never wear any sort of ring on the third finger of your left hand. Almost anything can look like an engagement ring or wedding band. You'd be amazed at how many single women wear a family heirloom or other ring on the "wrong" finger, then wonder why men don't approach them. You may know you're not spoken for; the rest of the world won't.

Men: demonstrate safety. It's not surprising that one of the most important concerns women have in meeting new men is for their own safety. You can't just come out and casually mention that you're not a convicted felon who's recently escaped from maximum security. You must demonstrate to the woman that you can be trusted, and you simply can't sound forced or artificial. Try making some statement about an activity with your family, or with a church or other organization. Something like, "I took my nephew to a ball game last week," or "This Saturday, I'm going to help my brother-in-law put in a new fence," will go a long way toward establishing you as a Nice Guy.

THE DANGERS OF BEING SECRETIVE

When you volunteer information about yourself, you're giving the other person a better picture of who you are. You're being open and honest. The other person won't have to probe you for more information--or leave wishing that he or she had. You'll put your counterpart at ease, and enable him or her to relax and open up. The conversation will go much more smoothly and naturally. On the other hand, if you clam up at an important moment, the other person will think that you have something to hide. (A natural assumption.)

After all, how can two people have a natural dialogue when each is constantly wondering why the other is alone, whether the person is normal, and/or whether or not they should enjoy the conversation or get the hell out of there? You'll both be carrying on two conversations--an external one with your new acquaintance, and an internal monologue that will only spark mistrust. In such a setting, the first conversation always suffers.

Don't let that happen.

CHAPTER 12:
Make Your Imagination Your Asset

We've all had the experience of letting our imagination "get the better of us." All too often, we picture a series of worst-case scenarios (bad dates, unhappy endings, rejection). Often, the reason we think such negative thoughts is that we recall a past hurt (or two, or ten) and imagine that a risk we're currently taking, or currently considering taking, will leave us in the same sorry state.

But that isn't the only thing our imaginations can do.

Imagination can conjure up success stories, too. Like when you have two of the "pick four" numbers so far in the lottery; as the television announces the third number, don't you imagine all the things you could do if you won the jackpot? Or when you're walking home from a good movie; don't you sometimes dream about what it would be like to be Tom Selleck or Kathleen Turner? Or perhaps you had a bad day at work; do you ever write a little script in which you pass along your resignation, and your boss begs you to stay?

So why not use your imagination to picture *good* things happening in your dating life? Try it now. Picture a social situation where you're comfortable and relaxed. You're looking and feeling your best, you're smiling, and you're saying all those witty things you usually think of after you leave parties, and wish you had said while you were still there. Imagine others at the party seeing you as an intriguing and outgoing person--an enjoyable person to be with. People are hanging around you instead of the onion dip. You're having a great time.

Stop here. Do not continue reading until you have really done this. Just reading about it isn't the same as doing it.

Now that you have a vivid mental picture of a socially

successful you, surrounded by people who think you're wonderful, save that picture and use the image when you really *are* at a party or other social gathering.

When Jody is "on the lookout" for a potential date, she starts by telling everyone that she's dating--long before she has even one date. She imagines herself in her dating mode. She lies in bed, imagining she has just met a wonderful sexy lover. She pictures where they met, where they went on their first date, even what she wore. The quiet little French restaurant and the black silk dress may not really exist, but she never lets that get in the way of her fantasy. Then she takes that warm and wonderful feeling of romantic anticipation with her into the real world. She imagines being more aggressive and creative about meeting men--and less afraid to make conversation with guys she's never met.

People in sales have long been aware of this technique. They picture themselves selling widget after widget, answering tricky questions perfectly, conveying sincerity and trust. They picture themselves closing the deal--actually writing up the sales slip. They do all this over and over again. And sure enough, those who are best at this technique (often called "creative visualization") are the ones who are most successful.

The same goes for athletes. Competitive divers, for example, will go over their routines again and again in their minds, feel every step on the board, the exact amount of lift they get as they spring off, visualize every twist and turn necessary to execute that perfect double somersault in a pike position . . . and then see a row of cards bearing the number ten go up at the judges' table. And the technique is apparently just as successful for athletes as it is for salespeople.

Why does it help? Who knows? Does it matter? The point is that *positive affirmations work*--and you can make them work for you, too.

A SECRET WEAPON

Do you have a friend who thinks you're super? Who knows you can do anything you set your mind to? Who believes in you wholeheartedly? Who thinks you're funny and clever and a blast to be around? Wouldn't it be great if this friend could somehow shrink to the size of a carpenter ant and hide behind your ear in social situations, cheering you on when you most need it?

Why not imagine your friend is with you, invisible to everyone else, encouraging you at every step. Picture what your friend might say to you in a discussion of the current situation. What would this friend suggest that you say or do? How would your friend react if given the same sets of choices you have? What would your friend tell you that would make you feel more confident?

If no such friends come to mind right away, try picturing an old lover who thought you were the hottest thing since salsa. Imagine the lover telling you exactly what makes you such a spicy dish.

Another, even better option is to try going out with that friend. Some people get noticeably more courageous when they're with someone who'll push them on to greatness. Maybe you could even make a contest out of the event: how many people can you smile at and say hello to in one night? In any event, you're looking for the kind of friend who'll say, "Aw, go on over there and say hello." The kind of friend you'll listen to.

Ralph got divorced after twenty years of marriage, and found talking to new women very difficult. His fear of rejection made it almost impossible for him to be assertive. Finally, his sister began dragging him to functions and even got him to dance. She'd stand next to him and say, "Ralph, that woman is smiling at you. Go ask that one with the red hair to dance." Ralph found that even when he stopped bringing his sister to social functions, he continued to imagine she was there by his side, saying, "Ralph, look over there. I think that one likes you."

WARNING

There's a big difference between making imagination your asset and setting yourself up to be disappointed. Don't make your fantasies so specific that you end up feeling let down when your dreams don't materialize exactly as you'd imagined.

For example, don't imagine that this blind date will be the date of your dreams, or that you'll definitely meet the perfect mate at next Tuesday night's party. You don't have any control over those events. Zero in on what *is* within your control. Imagine you will have a great time at a party, and that you'll dance to your heart's desire.

Kelly used visualization before going to a big party, and she did indeed meet an unattached guy she considered a knockout. She spent some time talking with him, and though they didn't exchange phone numbers, she was ecstatic--because her heart was pounding with excitement, and she felt "on" for the first time in months. Allowing herself to enjoy the moment helped build her confidence for the next encounter.

Think about the kids in Peter Pan. How did they learn to fly? They thought lovely thoughts, and up they went. No one's suggesting that the power of positive thinking will allow you to fly--but creative visualization may just help you negotiate obstacles a little better here on earth.

CHAPTER 13:
Find Places Where You're Comfortable Going Alone

The first rule you have to face about going out alone will tell you a lot about why people don't do it more often. Rule Number One reads as follows: "The first half hour stinks."

As you're sitting there feeling stupid, wondering when something interesting is going to happen, and wishing you had someone to talk to, you're bound to ask yourself several things. Why did I bother? Who on earth am I going to talk to? Why did I wear this? Who in their right mind would want to talk to someone who doesn't have someone to talk to and who's wearing what I'm wearing?

You will need at least thirty minutes to get over all this. That's about how long it will take you to be able to say to yourself, "Here I am. I already paid for my drink, so I might as well stay and see what happens. What the hell."

This is the first sign of relaxation.

When you reach this stage, your expectations will have eased somewhat, and you'll stop watching the door for the dancing figure of The Perfect Person You Have Been Waiting For All Your Life, eager to whisk you away to Monaco. There's always the possibility this will happen, but don't expect it to. Even if the PPYHBWFAYL doesn't carry you away on a road of clouds, you still may well have done the right thing by going out alone.

It takes time to relax and adjust emotionally to your surroundings. Once you do, you can notice interesting things, make mental notes of your surroundings, lean back, and maybe even have a little fun.

Ted loves jazz. He goes to jazz bars early, so he's sure to get a seat, and always brings a newspaper so he'll have something to look at if he feels the need to take a few moments to himself to get into the right frame of mind. The bartenders recognize Ted, and always greet him warmly. (The fact that he's a generous tipper doesn't hurt, of course.) If another single person, male or female, is seated next to Ted, the bartenders often introduce them. Two people who love jazz always have something to talk about, so Ted has an easy time meeting lots of new people this way. He feels comfortable at the jazz bars, because he's familiar with the environment, and never feels pressured to think of something to say. And even if there's no one to talk to, Ted always has a great time listening.

Of course, it's not only the jazz buffs who have plenty of material for conversation. The same goes for people who love country music, rock, boating, skiing, bowling, antiques, gourmet foods, books, animals, and just about any other special interest or hobby.

Check out your neighborhood. Look for the kind of place where you can stop by and be recognized when you simply have to get out of the house and don't know where else to go alone. It doesn't have to be a bar; you could pick a health club, a bowling alley, a bridge club--anyplace people meet in the evenings. If you do choose a bar, avoid the "meat market" types. Pick a quiet, friendly place where you can talk to the person sitting next to you.

A BAD EXCUSE
"I don't know of a place like that in my area."

Get off your duff and find one! It's out there somewhere. Start reading the papers; talk to your neighbors; find out what's happening of interest in your town. Get involved.

Keep in mind that, whether or not you meet a potential mate in the setting described here, you might meet a great friend. A new, brave, friend who's doing just what you're doing. You could support each other and provide mutual encouragement!

Maybe you'll meet someone whom you don't want to

date, but with whom you can have a great night of conversation. There's no law against that, is there? And remember: when you meet someone new, you widen your entire contact network.

You might also decide to go to the same place with a friend, but split up after you get there. Agree on the ground rules first: are you leaving together at 1 a.m., no matter what? Will you meet in the restroom at a certain time to tell each other how the night is going? What will the other person do if one of you meets someone?

The advantage of this approach is that you have the benefits of going someplace on your own--without really going on your own. You know you'll be able to talk to a friend at some point in the evening and compare notes, laugh at each others' stories, or get a pep talk that will boost your confidence.

GOING TO PARTIES ALONE

This is something you should think about, even if you're certain you won't know many people there besides the host or hostess. Consider Kate's approach.

Suzi and Bill invited Kate to their tenth anniversary party, held at a big nightclub. Kate knew lots of Suzi's and Bill's friends would be there, and that she wouldn't know most of them. The invitation specified formal dress. Normally, going to a party full of strangers gave Kate pause; the idea of going "stag" in an evening gown made her more nervous than usual. She went anyway--though it took some willpower. She felt as though she had to practically hurl herself through the door, and, true to Rule Number One, the opening minutes were no fun at all. The room was huge; when Kate finally spotted Suzi and Bill, they were on the dance floor, hardly the time to go over and say hello. While Kate waited through what must have been the longest dance number ever played, she talked back to the voices in her head telling her this was all wrong. That everyone was wondering where her date was or, worse, why she didn't have one. That women were looking at her dress and snickering. She began to sweat against velvet, leaving her feeling as though she were wearing a wet throw rug. Eventually Suzi and Bill "rescued" her--and introduced her to a group of people who all worked in the same office together and spent most of their time talking shop. After about thirty minutes of this (in accordance with Rule Number One), a man of about 75 years of age asked her to dance. To her surprise, she heard herself say yes. For some strange reason, that was the turning point. She relaxed, began to "fit in," and had a very nice dance with the older gentleman. Even more interesting, her dance card was full for the rest of the night!

Kate's experience illustrates a useful principle for those who go to parties alone. If someone asks you to dance, and you feel confident the asker is not someone you would end up dating, you have very little to lose, and a lot to gain, by saying yes.

The shy person in the corner will see you dancing and gain confidence. If you tell the non-date no, the shy person in the corner might think you considered the non-date too tall (or short, or plain, or weird), and that you would reject an invitation from him or her on the same grounds. (Of course, there's no reason you can't, after a few dances, get up enough nerve to go over to the shy person in the corner and issue an invitation of your own!)

Another good guideline to follow when you're alone at a party: if you ask someone to dance and the person turns you down, *ask someone else!*

THE TRUTH ABOUT BARS

You may hear from time to time that it's impossible to meet someone special in a bar. *This is a myth.* Nice people really do meet in bars--especially when they're not sending out frantic, "gee-I-hope-I-meet-someone" messages. It bears repeating: relaxed, confident people are more attractive than anxious, insecure ones, no matter where they are.

Jackie went to a singles bar with a friend on the way home from the movies one night. She just wanted to have a quick beer and watch the people, but her friend ended up talking to a cute guy. Just to occupy her time, Jackie started talking to the guy's friend, Martin, a journalist who was leaving for Sweden in a month on a long assignment. Jackie and Martin clicked, and subsequently made an attempt at an entry in the Guinness Book of World Records for the highest overseas phone bills ever recorded!

CHAPTER 14:
Learn a Few Good (Clean) Jokes or Tell a Great Story

Humor is one of the best ways to dissipate anxiety. It's also great for encouraging people to start talking, and it's a terrific method of focusing positive attention on yourself.

Peter went to a wedding reception where few of the guests at his table knew each other. The small talk, liberally peppered with long pauses, was going nowhere; people seemed uncomfortable. Peter decided to liven things up. Gesturing toward the head table, Peter said to the group, "You know, these guys are lucky. Did you hear what happened last month to the bride who was hijacked on the way to the church by robbers who commandeered the limo as a getaway car?" He proceeded to tell a funny story (with a happy ending, of course) that he'd read in the papers recently. The whole table came alive as people started imagining what it must have been like to be at *that* wedding. Comments came from around the table; before too long the whole group was in stitches.

Of course, humor *can* backfire. If someone is unfamiliar with your sense of what's funny, you can easily hurt his or her feelings. You may or may not get a second chance to explain that you didn't mean to be cruel.

Don't tell jokes that make fun of ethnic groups. It's even a good idea to avoid making fun of people's political views. How do you know who agrees with you on what? Just because the person you're talking to doesn't *look* like an Italian Republican whose dog has a limp, humor offensive to *any* group is a bad idea. First of all, you may be wrong in your assessment of your companion. And second of all, these days there's a good chance the listener may be offended no matter *what* his or her ancestry or inclination.

You should also guard against gutter-mouth or off-color humor, at least at the beginning stages of your acquaintance with someone. Springing the latest "blue" joke on someone who's unprepared for it is a good way to bring things to a screeching halt. No matter how funny you think a given joke is, steer away from it at the beginning of a meeting if the humor is sexually oriented.

Practice your jokes. Almost all professional comedians do, even the remarks that may seem off-the-cuff in concert. Why should you assume you don't need to? Tell your jokes to your best friend, your co-workers, or even to the mirror. Sharpen both your delivery and the joke's content. Try to do this with a number of jokes, so you can build an effective repertoire.

THE FIRST BAD EXCUSE

"I hardly ever hear any good jokes, and when I do, I never remember them when I want to tell them."

This shouldn't stop you. When you do hear a good joke you think you might want to tell later, *write it down* as soon as you can. Sometimes that will be enough to commit it to memory. If you don't hear lots of jokes, check your local bookstore for humor titles, or watch a good comedy show on television. Get out there and *find* the jokes.

STORIES

Jokes shouldn't be the only weapons in your arsenal. Everyone has had a couple of great adventures in life; some of them can even be told in public. Tell some of yours, even if they happened ages ago. Lean over and establish that you have a good story to tell. Use a tone of voice that sets a dramatic mood, and start the tale.

Ross--a very gentle literary type--survived six weeks of boot camp in the Marine Corps. He's the last person you'd expect to have joined the armed forces, but join he did, and the experience gave him material for tons of stories, funny and not-so-funny. Whenever he senses a lull in the conversation with someone new, Ross will say, "Let me ask you something. Do I look to you like the kind of guy who would join the Marines? Well, I did. That first trip to Parris Island had to be the most unnerving experience of my life . . ."

Shelly says to a man she's just met, "See that man over there? He looks positively criminal, but he doesn't scare me. I don't scare easily any more. Not after what happened to me a few summers ago in Greece . . ." She then relates how she was wrongfully accused of stealing a ring by a crazy woman while she was on vacation--and how she didn't speak a word of Greek at the time!

THE SECOND BAD EXCUSE

"My life's been really ordinary. I don't have any exciting stories to tell."

Unlikely. But for the sake of argument, let's assume it's true. No problem; all you have to do is tell a great story that happened to someone else! (That's what Peter did at the wedding reception, remember?) You don't even have to pretend the story happened to you. The point is simply to pass along a fascinating event.

A nice variation on the above is to try to draw others out by getting them to tell you *their* stories. For example, if you were Shelly in the example above, you might conclude by asking, "What's the scariest thing that's ever happened to *you*?"

CHAPTER 15:
Make New Friends
of Both Sexes

Don't misunderstand. Your current friends are wonderful. What would you do without them? Who would you call when your water heater breaks down when it's least convenient? Who would commiserate with you when your heart has been broken by the same lover for the fourteenth time, and everyone else is sick of hearing about it?

Old friends share your history, your values, and, often, a certain common outlook. They often echo your thoughts and feelings. But even so, there's something to be said for making new acquaintances--not to replace the old relationships, but to expand the "pool" of people you know. And who knows? Another *great* friend may be out there waiting to be discovered!

Try finding new friends--both men and women--who are socially outgoing, and who are likely to inspire you to great leaps of confidence. Look for people who remind you, by their very presence, that to have a good time you have to *be* a good time.

Meeting new people can bring out some of the best parts of your personality. When you make new friends, you usually put on the polish, and that witty and charming person waiting within you to be released sees fit to make an appearance. Remember that commercial for spaghetti sauce that issues the constant refrain, "It's in there"? Making new friends--outside of a romantic context--is a great way to remind yourself how attractive your "hidden" personality can be. It's in there, make no mistake.

Michelle went to a poetry reading with her new friend Debbie. After the reading, there was a reception. Michelle and Debbie split up and met several people independently. When Michelle wanted to leave and went to say goodbye to Debbie, Debbie had other ideas. Debbie had met a magazine editor who wanted them all to go out for a drink. Michelle protested, but in vain. It was a good thing Debbie insisted--Michelle had a great time, and the three even went out dancing afterwards!

You should get to know a Debbie. Debbie is the person who calls you up and says, "I refuse to let you spend another night in front of the tube. I don't care how tired you are. Find something nice to wear and meet me in half an hour." Debbie is the one who gets tickets to the new art gallery opening, or who finds out about an old-fashioned hootenanny, or who signs you both up for a cruise. Debbies are essential; every home should have one.

So: where do you find a Debbie (or a Donald)? Anywhere, really. Strike up a conversation with someone in your office whom you've always thought was terrific, someone you've been wanting to go out to lunch with for a long time. Go talk to the person who just moved into your building; after all, you say hi every week in the laundry room. Join a workshop. Take a class. Sign up for a committee. All of these are excellent ideas for getting in contact with potential dates, of course, but you shouldn't limit yourself to that. Great friends are important, too.

You can, of course, abandon any activity you undertake or group you join later on if you find it boring or unproductive. Try to involve yourself in settings that will expose you to new non-romantic friendships.

When Cassandra first moved to New York, she knew only one person. She joined a writers' workshop right away. One night, her new friends invited her to a party, where she met a number of *their* friends. Within a week, she had come in contact with thirty new people, and had made more than one friendship that was to last for several years.

If your new friendship fizzles--if Juanita breaks your lunch date at the last minute and never calls back, or if Tony falls madly in love and refuses to spend time away from his girlfriend--accept it, and don't take anything personally. Call someone else.

"WHAT'S WITH YOU LATELY?"

A word of warning: some of your old friends may not like all this. They may begin to feel left out when your life shows signs of changing. If Nick is used to getting a call from you every Friday night, and suddenly you're not home on Friday nights, he may begin to feel left out. He may even tell you the "new you" is frivolous. Listen to what your friend has to say. Respect his opinion. *But don't let him hold you back.*

Entering new adventures involves risk. If you're already feeling a trifle anxious or uneasy with your new, adventurous self, you might let someone talk you out of your new initiatives. There might even be a part of you that wants to give up and take it easy again. *Don't do it.* If you want to listen to an old friend's what's-gotten-into-you-lately lecture, go ahead and listen. Keep your ears open for constructive criticism, but then *go out and do what you were going to do anyway.*

KEEPING AN OPEN MIND

You might even consider turning the wrong lover into the right friend. When you meet people you like, but don't think are right for you romantically, there's absolutely nothing wrong with enlarging your circle of friends. Just make it clear that friendship is what you're after; don't mislead anyone.

Building friendships will expand your contact network of people who might know potential lovers, but it will enrich your single life in other ways, too. Strong friendships offer you the opportunity to do a little reality testing and compare a few notes. How does one decide who picks up the check these days? Will your date overreact if you invite him to dinner with your family? Would slipping a note under her door scare the woman you'd like to meet who lives in your apartment building? Talk it over in confidence; you'll probably both get something out of it.

Opposite-sex friends also serve as great last-minute

dates for occasions that seem to preclude your going alone. In this and many other ways, your non-signficant other can help you significantly.

CHAPTER 16:
Create a
Buddy System

Remember when you were at summer camp, and the counselor wouldn't let you go into the deep water, or into the forest, or anyplace else that seemed at all risky without having a buddy along? Your buddy was there just in case something Went Wrong, and if you're like most of us, just having the buddy there made you feel a little safer.

You can use the same principle today *without* having to sew name tags on your underwear. Creating a buddy system as an adult helps you keep yourself in circulation and provides a "safety net" that encourages you to try new ways of meeting people. You'll probably also notice that, after a while, it's difficult to offer up the same timeworn complaints to your buddy about how hard it is to find the right person. This is certainly a positive development, considering how easy it is for most of us to lapse into unproductive cycles by replaying such complaints endlessly.

Betsy and Diane have a buddy system that works. When they go to a dance or nightclub together, they agree ahead of time to separate when they get through the door, and meet in the ladies' room at quarter to eleven. What's more, they agree that they must each talk to at least ten new people of either sex, and ask a minimum of five men to dance. This provides a feeling of unity, one that's bolstered by their constant mutual praise and support. Their system relieves a lot of the anxiety that accompanies "getting yourself out there." The nicest thing is that they're both going on more dates since they started their "collaboration."

Not all buddies have to be same-sex buddies, of course. Consider Noah and Emily's case.

Noah feels he can use a little advice about women now and then, and Emily sometimes finds herself in need of some pointers on men. They regularly swap suggestions. Perhaps the most unusual aspect of their relationship is that they aren't particularly close friends. They met through the personals section of a local newspaper, and didn't really hit it off as dating partners. So now they've struck a different sort of partnership--one that's invaluable to both of them. Every week, they talk on the phone to discuss what each is planning and to see how the other person is coming along. Having someone else to report to provides both Noah and Emily with the gentle push each needs to stay motivated.

Don't use the buddy system as a form of competition. The point isn't to outdo someone by meeting more people, getting more dates, or going to more places. The point is to provide mutual support. So don't keep score.

Almost anyone can be a buddy, but sometimes buddy systems work best when you choose a new friend, rather than someone you already know. You may find that, in such a setting, you'll be more likely to stick with the system, since the system itself is the basis of your new friendship. With someone you already see periodically, you may be more likely to taper off into unproductive habits.

When you pick a buddy, pick someone with a positive, upbeat attitude. Your buddy is your support system. Make sure the connection is a solid one, and the person is someone you can count on. That doesn't mean you shouldn't expect your buddy to get disappointed or even downright grumpy from time to time. That's how the system works; each of you is there when the other needs a pep talk. But if your buddy spends significantly more time complaining about dating problems than helping you both come up with new ideas for solving those problems, re-evaluate your friend's contributions to the buddy relationship.

CALL YOUR BUDDY

When you feel a little unsure, when your environment seems a bit threatening, when it seems you're in over your head, call your buddy. When you're not sure what Diane meant when she said she couldn't go out with you Friday night because her astrologer advised against it, call your buddy. When you think it's hard to stay motivated, but you *don't* want to stay home and mope, call your buddy. You'll be back in the swing of things before you know it.

CHAPTER 17:
Learn to Transfer
Your Skills

Sylvia is a stylish and striking woman who leaves an unforgettable impression. She runs a successful dating service that matches up hundreds of couples every month. Yet Sylvia hasn't had a date in over a year. She's great at interviewing new people and making them feel relaxed and confident. She's always able to convince others to trust her. And she frequently organizes big parties for people who want to meet others. But she can't seem to meet men on her own. Sylvia is wonderful at taking care of someone else's problem, at getting others motivated--but she can't seem to do the same things for herself.

Joey works in the personnel department of a large company. He does a lot of recruiting, so he's always initiating conversations with strangers, as well as listening and responding to others in an engaging and supportive way. He's very good at those things, that is, until he tries to do something for himself instead of for his company. Then Joey freezes.

Does any of the above sound familiar? Are you able to negotiate a tough contract, teach a class of unruly sixth graders, calm an anxious patient, make cold calls to get new clients, tell your boss he's not being fair, or make a presentation to hundreds of strangers--yet unable to overcome being tongue-tied when it comes to your own social life?

Learn to transfer your skills. We all have at least one thing we're really good at. (Sure you do.) Think about what you do all day long, and how you might transfer the skills you need to accomplish that to your life as a single. Instead of groaning about what you're *not* good at, admit that you may not have assessed your skills appropriately and concentrate on what you *are* good at.

Don't just think about your professional life. Think about everything you do--as a community volunteer, class officer for the school reunion committee, member of the PTA, best cook on the block, or part-time poet. Don't skip any area of your life that might involve skills.

After you've done some serious thinking, fill out twin lists. They might look something like this.

I AM ABLE TO:
- . . . walk up to new colleagues and clients and introduce myself
- . . . take charge of a situation when necessary
- . . . do what needs to be done without having to be told to do it
- . . . take risks

I WANT TO BE ABLE TO:

- . . . walk up to strangers at a party and introduce myself
- . . . feel in control and not at the mercy of the whims of others
- . . . make myself responsible for meeting others
- . . . take risks

Many people underestimate their successes and overplay their failures. How many times have you read interviews with actors who say that, even though they got scores of good reviews, the one bad review they got is the one they remember?

Draw up your list and look closely at the skills you actually possess. By doing this, you'll learn to recognize your strengths and praise yourself for them. You'll project a stronger image.

SKILLS VS. ACCOMPLISHMENTS

A skill isn't the same thing as an accomplishment. The point of this exercise is to translate your talents, not flaunt your credentials or memorize your resume to impress people later on. While talking about accomplishments when you're in the dating "hotseat" can be a way of saying to someone that you're worth taking a look at, don't overdo it.

Chest-beating gets boring quite rapidly. Besides, making a sales pitch about your job (or anything else) will make you sound more like you're trying to close a big deal than get a date. Put your professional skills to use, but define yourself in broader terms than what you do for a living.

Now go sharpen your pencil and start your list. Keep it in a place where you can see it regularly, and use it your advantage--by remembering what you *can* do when that little voice in the back of your head insists on reciting things you supposedly *can't* do.

CHAPTER 18:
Buy Every Singles-Related Publication You Can Get Your Hands On

A recent singles/personals section in an issue of a major Boston magazine featured 210 advertisements. Of these, 66 were placed by women, 42 were placed by men, and 102 described opportunities for singles to meet each other!

That means there are a lot of resources you could be taking advantage of through these publications. Find the right happening, and you have one less excuse to spend Friday nights wondering when (and how) Don Johnson is going to get his hair streaked again.

Singles magazines and newsletters offer many interesting leads. You can find articles about intimacy and self-esteem, new perspectives on beating the "odds" associated with single life, as well as tons of personal ads that cost nothing to answer. Some even have lists of parties and events you might want to attend.

Keeping up with these publications is not the same thing as "answering personals." You'll come across those ads, of course, but you're just as likely to find out about parties, auctions, discussion groups, support networks for certain types of singles (such as the hearing impaired, divorced persons, or specific ethnic groups), networking opportunities, pen pals, countless sports and games nights ranging from volleyball and softball to Scruples and Trivial Pursuit, workshops, golden oldies nights, dances to which large and lovely people are expressly invited, dances for people in certain age groups, and much, much, more.

The point is, the perfect setting for your efforts to meet the right person may *already exist*, but unless you check the singles publications, you probably won't know that it's scheduled for this Saturday night at seven.

HOW TO KEEP TRACK OF IT ALL

Don't get too overwhelmed by the opportunities you'll learn about through singles papers. You don't have to attend *everything* this week. But gather as many as you can and *start a singles clipping file.*

File ads that seem interesting, even if you don't want to act on them right away. Maybe the club doesn't advertise in every issue; if that's the case, you won't be able to find contact information when you are interested unless you clip the listing now. Keep an organized file, not a stack of clippings that's likely to get mixed in with bills and other forgettable documents we tend to put aside for extended periods.

As we'll learn in a later chapter, it's a good idea to clip personal ads that you wish you'd written, even if they're placed by people of the "wrong" sex. If you ever decide to place an ad of your own, you'll have inspiration on file.

TAKING ADVANTAGE OF OPPORTUNITIES

Now that you have a singles clipping file, you'll be ready for those nights when you really want to go out, but have no particular place to go and are unable to find friends with a free evening.

You can dig into the file. line up all the possibilities, make a few phone calls--and go from having nothing to do to having dozens of interesting possibilities.

Caitlyn used to sit around on the weekends and wish she had something fun to do. Something unusual. Something more inviting and exotic than thinking about how she didn't want to clean up her apartment, a task she'd been known to brood over for weekends on end. In these situations, she would always remember having heard about an event or two that she was interested in, but never had the details at her fingertips. All that changed once she started her singles clipping file. She found, to her astonishment, that whenever she looked for new items for her file, she found many more than she could possibly attend. It was a pleasant surprise. Now Caitlyn has options, and free time with no set plans is no longer something she dreads. She's seldom without plans for very long. Lately, she's been concentrating on finding ways to clean her apartment more quickly and efficiently. She's got too many other interesting things to do with her time.

CHAPTER 19:
Get on Every Singles Mailing List You Can

Now that you've picked up all the singles publications you can find, and have looked through them to see what sort of groups and activities for singles your area offers, take the next step. Make sure you stay informed about such events and opportunities. Call up each of the groups your research unearths--and get on all the mailing lists you can.

A BAD EXCUSE

"But I've been to a few of their functions, and I didn't much care for the people I ran into."

Things change! Okay, so the Easter brunch brochure you got sent you on a mad dash for the circular file when you read the part about how "all boys dressed like Peter Rabbit and all girls dressed like Miss April will be admitted half price." Still--that doesn't mean that two weeks from now, the same group won't have discovered the error of its ways (or hired new management). Maybe the next event will feature Carl Sagan as a guest speaker. You never know. And anyway, what's wrong with getting mail? Just because you get an invitation doesn't mean you have to go.

The idea is to increase your options. Having more options gives you more choices. More control. More opportunities to meet people.

Try it. Put yourself on every singles mailing list you can find. Before long, your mailbox will probably be filled with two new and unusual categories of mail: requests for donations and invitations to meetings and parties.

Some of the activities will look great; others will be the type you'd never attend. But you may well find that one of the organizations on your "no way" list ends up sponsoring a volleyball game or other event you might enjoy.

Once you get on lots of mailing lists, and keep a file of

clippings from singles magazines, you'll have only one excuse for sitting at home: it's what you damn well feel like doing. And that's a great reason to stay home. *But if you don't want to sit around at home by yourself, you don't have to.*

DON'T BE FOOLED BY APPEARANCES

Be on the lookout for singles activities disguised as just-plain-everyday activities. When you're looking for lists to get your name on, you might not automatically consider university activities, sports clubs, or the YMCA or YWCA. These really do count as singles opportunities, however, because many of the participants are single and are eager to meet other singles.

Harriet spends time at the local boating club, offering to go out with experienced sailors who need or want company. She helps out as an extra deck hand, and they teach her about sailing and boating. The more experience she gets, the more people ask her to join them. Asking an experienced sailor for a few tips isn't the same as asking for a date, but this maneuver does win Harriet 30 minutes of uninterrupted time alone with a person she finds interesting--long enough to see if there's anything worth pursuing further, and short enough to keep from making a big investment.

Sally is more choosy than a lot of singles about what events she attends. She's not comfortable going to just any old party she learns about through a flyer in the mail. She uses her singles network and does some research. She asks friends and acquaintances if they've ever heard of the sponsor. She might also watch the sponsor's ads for a while to see if they advertise regularly; she feels better about groups that run ads repeatedly, as it shows stability and a concern for repeat business. If she has a phone number, she calls the place in question to see what kind of person answers. She asks questions: what age range usually attends the events, how many people usually show up? She eliminates some places right away.

Whether or not you attend even one event, being on all these mailing lists is guaranteed to do at least two things for you. It will increase the amount of trash you have to take out each week, and it will motivate you to get out there--by reminding you that there is an out there into which you can get.

Even if you see an ad for a pool party, and pool parties have always been all wet in your estimation, call the group and ask to get on its list. Next month they might have a midnight cruise (or limbo tournament, or French cooking demonstration, or golden oldies band) that *does* interest you. And if you're not on the list, you might not hear about it.

CHAPTER 20:
Walk Your Pet (Borrow One If You Have To)

Nancy walks home through Manhattan's Central Park every afternoon. She sees the same man with the same dog in the same spot every day. And every time Nancy sees the man, he's talking to a different woman.

Pets are wonderful companions; they are also terrific tools for meeting people. They're living, breathing conversation pieces. Even people who are in a rotten mood usually have a soft spot in their hearts for animals.

Stopping to pat a cocker spaniel or a dachshund or a black cat with white paws is not only unthreatening, it's also positively therapeutic. The unconditional love animals give people is habit-forming. After all, do you know anyone who couldn't use a little more unconditional love?

Pets in social settings tend to reduce perceived risk. When you have a pet in tow, people you approach will probably think, "How bad could that person be? After all, he (she) is an animal lover." You become more interesting, less threatening, and more caring than the average person one might meet in a bar.

A BAD EXCUSE
"But I don't own a pet, and I'm not about to buy one just to make meeting other singles easier."

Borrow one from a friend!

Arthur is a very handsome man, well-built with blue eyes. He is also extremely shy. He doesn't have a pet, but one Saturday afternoon he borrowed an English sheepdog named Waldo from a friend and took the animal for a walk in a busy area of Boston. Women stopped to talk to Waldo, and when they had exhausted their conversation with him, they talked to Arthur. Waldo somehow put these women in a warm, friendly mood. Arthur began to get better at talking to people that day; he and Waldo spend quite a few Saturday mornings together now. Only mornings, though. These days, the rest of Arthur's weekend is usually occupied.

A basset hound. A cat. A parrot on your shoulder. Pets come in a bewildering array of shapes and sizes--find one that's right for you. Be inventive (Knowledgeable sources have it that the in thing these days in Los Angeles is to walk your snake, though this sounds like slow going.)

DON'T GET SIDETRACKED
Be sure when you're out walking your pet that you get to know other *people*, and not just their pets. Wouldn't it bruise your ego to have someone spend twenty minutes talking to your dog before even acknowledging your existence? (One woman we know is considering training her Yorkie to hand out her business card.)

If your pet has undergone a mishap recently, that's usually no reason to write this technique off. Animals with bandages or casts attract much more sympathy and attention than the rest of the field. For that matter, a dog with a "prop"--like a scarf around its neck--appears more friendly than an unadorned dog. What this basically comes down to is, pets with conversation pieces attract more people.

WHERE TO GO
Simply walking the pet isn't enough. You must choose the right place for your walk. If you walk the dog around your block every night, and you already know everyone on your block, you're not going to meet any new people.

Take your dog, cat, bird, snake, or iguana to a number of different places. Try the park first, then move on to shopping districts, main thoroughfares, summer outdoor concerts, or neighborhood softball games. Experiment!

Remember: unless your dog is spayed or neutered, it may find a lover before you do. This may or may not be a setback. It's entirely possible that you'll meet even more people walking the litter of puppies.

CHAPTER 21:
When Going to Bars, Plan Ahead

L et's face it. Trying to meet people in bars can be a harrowing experience. Fortunately, with a little advance planning, you can make the bar "scene" less threatening. You may not be able to mix martinis and margaritas, but, by thinking ahead, you can prove to yourself that the people who order them can go together quite nicely.

The first rule is to get there early. Try going at 5:30 pm on a weeknight. At that time of day, the clientele is not the same as the stereotypical bar crowd, and this will work to your advantage.

AT 5:30, PEOPLE . . .

. . . are just on their way home from work.

. . . are beginning to unwind.

. . . aren't shy or over-anxious, because they aren't planning to meet anyone.

. . . have no major expectations.

. . . are relaxing.

AT 11:00, PEOPLE . . .

. . . have already had one tequila sunrise too many.

. . . are getting nervous that they might not land the Big One that night.

. . . are generally strained and anxious, because they feel they're on display like something from "Ripley's Believe It or Not."

. . . may get antsy when they wonder if they should have gone to the other place because this bar isn't delivering.

. . . are strutting.

When you're deciding where to go, consider an establishment with live entertainment. That way, you'll have a neutral focus for your attention, as well as a reason for being there other than to meet people. What's more, you'll only have to be charming for twenty minutes at a time, when the band takes breaks.

Remember to bring your conversation piece!

WHAT HAPPENS IF YOU SEE SOMEONE INTERESTING?

So there you are, seated at the bar. You see someone interesting and attractive seated elsewhere, or standing at the the other side of the room. What do you so?

Plan A: Walk over and say hello.

Plan B: First, wait till he or she goes to the restroom. Then amble over in that direction as though you were looking for the restroom yourself. (This applies even if you've been to this place every Friday since you reached legal drinking age, and maybe a few before that, and know damn well where the restrooms are.) Just before you think he or she is due to come out, head for the restroom so you will be in the person's path when he or she emerges. (Doing this will require a little estimation on your part; adjust your timing depending on the sex of the person and the number of people you've seen going into the restroom recently.) Start a conversation.

You may not realize what an advantage following Plan B can be. But think about it. The person who has just come out of the restroom is always in a better mood than when he or she entered. You are approaching a person who is, so to speak, relieved. At least you know that if you start talking to the person, he or she won't suddenly bolt away on the pretense of having to use the restroom.

By now you're probably wondering to yourself, "What exactly am I supposed to say to someone who's just come out of the restroom? 'Did you have a nice time in there'?" Rest assured, you do have other options. Here are some examples.

> Oh, that's the *men*'s room. I thought it was the *ladies'* room. Good thing you stopped me or I might not have survived.

Oops. Wrong way. My direction is off, can you tell?

I thought this was the ladies' room: leave it to me to start a scene. Thanks. You wouldn't be able to point me in the right direction, would you?

(For the truly brave:) Hi. (Big smile.)

You may have other ideas of your own. Take a couple of minutes now to jot them down. Keep in mind that you're looking only for a two- or three-line exchange . . . not a whole discussion.

At any rate. There you are in front of the rest room, having exchanged a few words with this interesting person. You've made yourself familiar. The two of you smile and go your separate ways, but you've established a contact of sorts. You can walk over to the person a little later and say something like, "Hey, that's a nice tie. Where'd you get it?"

OTHER METHODS

If you don't like the restroom strategy, here are some more ideas.

Sit near the attractive person and say, "Pass the peanuts please," then smile as he or she does so. (If there are no peanuts, you might consider the direct approach: buy a bag of peanuts, place them in front of the person, then say, "Pass the peanuts." Not for the faint of heart.)

Send over a drink (but peek at Chapter 43 first).

Go play a video game. Someone who's been watching you (or maybe even winking at you), but is too shy to come over in front of your seven friends, might just muster up the necessary courage to come over and start a discussion about your alien-blasting technique. (Pop quiz: what does the video game become in this example? If you don't know the answer, start reading this book again from chapter one. Hint, hint.)

CHAPTER 22: Browse Through the Apparel Department (for the Opposite Gender) of a Classy Retail Store

Maria's old friend Ron asked her to go to a fashionable men's store with him during a big Saturday sale to help pick out a winter coat. Maria wasn't really excited about the prospect, especially since she liked to sleep in on weekends, and Ron wanted to get there early while the pickings were good. But Ron convinced her, and off they went. What Maria didn't consider was the possibility that the store might be overstocked with men of all ages and sizes, which indeed it was. Her interest picked up shortly after they arrived. Maria saw the name of a men's designer she admired and walked over to chat with a man who was browsing through a rack of cashmere sweaters. "I'd stick with the green," she offered casually. "It's a great shade." The sweater-browser smiled, and the two began a discussion of current fashions for men. Before long, she realized that Ron had actually done her quite a favor by "dragging her along" that morning!

Part of the reason this technique works so well is that people's defenses are often down when they shop for clothes. It's somehow easier to talk; no one is expecting to meet someone in a store. It's unlikely that someone would be nervous or anxious in such a situation. You'll probably be less nervous than in other "encounter" situations, too, since you're taking less of a risk in initiating conversation than you would at, say, a dance.

A good general rule is, the nicer the store, the more well-heeled the clientele. In other words, Woolworth's is great if you want to date Minnie Pearl.

You have several ways of going about meeting people in this manner. Offering your opinion to a person who seems undecided, as Maria did, is one way. *Asking* for an opinion is another.

> *You:* Excuse me. I'm looking for something special for my sister--she just had her first baby, and I want to surprise her with something really pretty. Do you think a sweater like this would be a good idea, or should I stick with something like these rainbow colored socks?
>
> *Intriguing Female Stranger:* Well, I never had a baby, so I'm not sure exactly what a new mother would like best. But somehow a sweater seems better than the socks. I don't know, it just seems more feminine and personal. I saw some great colors over here . . .

Here's another example.

> *You:* Excuse me. I'm looking at this pullover for my father. It was his birthday last week, and I'm late as usual with a gift, so I want to get him something really nice. He's about your size. You think this would fit?
>
> *Intriguing Male Stranger:* Let's see the tag. I usually wear a large, and this is a medium. If your dad has really broad shoulders, this might not fit him. I think I saw some larges over on that table. . .

The point is to give the person some background first. Make yourself human. Present other information about your life. In the above examples, the Intriguing Strangers now know you have a family about which you care quite a bit. They know you want to make the people you love happy. They know you care enough about others to spend some time on them, rather than taking the easy way out. It's a small point (and you shouldn't overdo the real-person background), but these pieces of information can be important in making a positive impression.

Even if you don't exchange phone numbers, you've still had the chance to hone your social skills by talking with someone else. It's a no-lose situation.

Men: try the perfume or cosmetics counter, too. Isn't that where Robin Williams met Maria Conchita Alonso in "Moscow on the Hudson"?

Women: try doing the same thing at a stereo store; such outlets usually attract more male customers than female ones.

Retail stores are not only good for meeting new people; they're also quite effective as settings in which to get to know someone better.

Kathy wanted to go out with Sam, but he hadn't asked her yet, and she was too shy to ask him. She knew, though, that if they got to know one another, they'd hit it off well. Then she had a stroke of brilliance. Instead of calling him and asking him for a date, she asked if he'd go with her to help her pick out some good stereo equipment. Her request provided them with a goal, a task to complete, a reason for getting together--and something else to concentrate on besides how well they were or weren't doing in making a good impression. Yet the task also gave them the time and opportunity to get to know one another, since they ended up talking about lots of things that had nothing to do with stereo equipment!

If you think about it, you can probably come up with lots of other unorthodox places where you stand a pretty good chance of meeting new people in a non-threatening atmosphere. Waiting in line for stamps at the post office; in the waiting area of a travel agent's office; at the motor vehicle registry; the possibilities are endless.

Don't assume that you have to go shopping in order to meet nice people (though, if you do, you'll probably have more friends to complain to when the next Visa bill arrives).

CHAPTER 23:
Spend Time in Bookstores, Video Stores, and Libraries

It happened completely by accident. Ross was on his knees in the bookstore aisle because he was looking for a book by an author whose last name began with a "W." At the same time, a woman by the opposite shelf was on her tiptoes, trying to dislodge a title just out of her reach. She lost her balance, fell backwards, and landed on Ross. She apologized profusely, and asked if Ross was hurt. He said he was fine--then asked her what book was so important to her that she'd risk life and limb for it. She laughed, and told him about her interest in detective stories. Ross asked if she'd seen the recent PBS special on the subject. They talked for a while, then decided to go out for coffee.

You might fall for someone in a bookstore, but you certainly don't have to fall *on* the person to make an impression. Start by browsing. Pick up different books and magazines; flip through them.

Notice other browsers, and watch what they're looking at. After you've browsed some more, ask someone about a book you're interested in (or about what the person is reading at the moment). See what happens.

Gina decided that, after all the hoopla over *Women Who Love Too Much*, she really ought to read the book. She went into a bookstore and picked up a copy. As she walked to the register, a man near her, who'd seen her select the book,

asked, "Where's the book, *Men Who Love Too Much*?"
Gina smiled and piped back, "In the fantasy section."   He
joined her in line, and the two started talking about the
book.

Self-help books make good conversation starters. So do
classics like Joyce's *Ulysses*, though you shouldn't try to fake
your way through a discussion of such books without
having read them. (You'll probably be spotted a mile off.)
Also consider titles that have a loyal "cult" following, like
One Hundred Years of Solitude by Marquez.

People often find it easier to start a conversation about a
book they have an opinion about. (Be careful, though: don't
let a lively, interesting debate turn into a nasty argument.)

Watch the newspapers, and note when authors are going
to be signing copies of books at a local bookstore. If you
like the person's work, this can be an excellent event to
attend; the people you'll meet will already share an interest
with you, the author's work. Striking up a conversation in
such a setting is quite easy, and you might even follow
things up with an invitation for coffee afterwards.

The bookstore around the corner is beginning to look like a
singles party on Friday nights, Steven thought to himself.
Some of the faces *were* distinctly familiar from week to
week. So he took the plunge himself. One night after work,
he walked in and began watching the clientele as he
browsed. He worked up his courage and approached a
woman in the mystery section. "I saw you buying the new
Dick Francis mystery a few weeks back," he said. "I noticed
because I'm a fan of his from way back, but I haven't had
the time to read that one yet. Did you like it?"   She had
liked it. And, as it turned out, she liked Steven as well.

Of course, you won't always meet a fascinating person
who thinks you're fascinating too. If you try the bookstore
route once, and don't succeed, don't decide the idea stinks
based on one try. Keep at it.

If you talk to someone who interests you, but who doesn't return the interest, you'll still feel better for having taken the initiative and for giving it a try. The next time will be that much easier. (You may even pick up a good book out of the exercise.)

VIDEO, VIDEO, AND OTHER IDEAS

Video stores offer similar opportunities. Many of the people browsing through them on Friday nights are single, just like you, and looking, just like you, for an entertaining way to spend the evening. Ask an interesting person about the movie he or she is holding. Ask if the person has seen the movie you're thinking of renting.

Sunday afternoons in the library reading room provide still more opportunities. Ask the person who catches your eye to let you read the paper when he or she is finished . . . then ask how your favorite column was this week. If the person has read the column, voila--you'll have something to discuss. If not, don't panic; you can still talk about why you like to follow the column. This is a win-win proposition unless the librarian walks over and tells you to put a lid on it.

The library's bookshelves, and the line at the check-out counter, also present opportunities for you to talk to others and ask them what they're reading, whether they like it, and what you think of what you're reading.

Most libraries also have all kinds of programs you can take advantage of--lectures, readings, speakers, exhibitions and such--and they're usually free. Call your library and ask what events are scheduled. Find out if the library has a mailing list; if so, ask to be included in it. Learn all you can about events that interesting people might attend--then go.

CHAPTER 24:
Go To A Trade Show, Convention, Auction, Or Sale

Lorna makes beautiful macrame belts. She went to a fashion accessory trade show in New York City (where she lived) to try to sell them. She stopped at one of the booths when she saw a great looking guy behind the table. His name was Mike. They talked for a few minutes, and she learned he lived in Buffalo. Too far away, she thought sadly, and left politely. But the next day, she found herself at the talking to the same man--he had come to her booth this time. They seemed to be hitting it off. Lorna wasn't seeing anyone, and she really enjoyed talking to Mike; when he asked for her phone number, she was surprised to hear herself give it to him. Mike travels to New York on business quite a bit, and he and Lorna have been seeing each other for over a year now. Sometimes she even makes it into Buffalo.

If you live in or near a major urban area, it's a sure bet that you have access to trade shows and conventions for just about everything. You should also keep an eye out for auctions and special sales that attract people with specific interests. Choose events that are most likely to attract the types of people you want to meet.

You must read the paper, or you'll never learn about these events. Radio and television stations sometimes advertise upcoming opportunities, but the best resource is definitely your newspaper.

Here are some ideas for places to start.

A record sale or record collectors' convention. (For music lovers.)
A rare book sale. (For literary types.)
A boat show or rare car show. (For people who want to meet someone with a few bucks.)
An exercise equipment show or health food and nutrition conference. (For health enthusiasts.)
A computer and electronics show. (For techies.)
An old comic book sale. (For Spider-Man fans.)

You can meet people of all kinds while you wander through conventions, conferences, auctions, and sales. Sure, some of the people you run into will fit the party-hat-and-toy-horn stereotype of the convention-goer, but that's usually late at night after the third martini (theirs, not yours).

Don't limit yourself to your own neighborhood--check the newspapers of nearby towns, too. Don't pass up something wonderful just because you have to put 50 miles on your car's odometer to get there.

So remember. If you've got nothing better to do on a Sunday afternoon, put on your best clothes and go test drive a Porsche at that big foreign car sale you read about. Even if you don't meet anyone interesting, driving that cherry-red Porsche, and forgetting for the moment about your 1969 Volkswagen Beetle, may well give you the material for that great story you've been looking for since Chapter 14.

CHAPTER 25:
Learn to Work at Your Own Level Of Comfort

Finding a lover is a process. There is no single suggestion you can take from this book that will automatically change your love life in a dramatic way. In short, there is no magic trick--it will probably take time for things to evolve.

You might walk out the door tomorrow and bump into the person of your dreams. That really does happen. But what's more likely is that the opportunity will come from something you generate. And the best way to generate opportunities is to be open, friendly, and available, even when doing so seems unlikely to lead to a direct hit.

How you take the steps necessary to find the right lover is up to you. Each of us has a slightly different idea about how we want to accomplish that goal, of course; no one can say what's most comfortable for you. So work at your own pace.

On the one hand, you don't want to box yourself in by making unnecessary rules like, "I'm not the type to wear a leather skirt," or, "I'm not the type to say hello first." By the same token, though, you don't want to stretch yourself so far that you lose your sense of self and end up trying to be someone you're not. If you put yourself under the constant strain and pressure of attaining your goal, you won't have any fun--and, ultimately, your very efforts will be one of the reasons you won't succeed in meeting the people you want to meet. People will sense the pressure you place on yourself, and won't want to get close to you.

Alma's friends kept telling her to be more aggressive in meeting men--to wear sexier clothes, offer her phone number first, approach interesting strangers at nightclubs, and so on. But Alma was uncomfortable trying to do this. She hated nightclubs, and felt really dumb whenever she let her friends pressure her into trying to be what they called a modern woman. Their strategies worked for them, but they succeeded only in humiliating Alma. Finally, she got so frustrated that she stopped trying to please everyone else, and concentrated on being who she really was. And a funny thing happened. Alma had a streak of good luck. When she was relaxed and acting like herself, she met more men--men who liked Alma because she liked herself.

Having people tell you what you should be doing and how many nights a week you should be doing it can be rough. To read some of the magazines on the newsstands these days, you'd think everyone was wrapped up in a social whirl night after night after night--and if that's the case, shouldn't you be seeing a lot more stooped, hung-over people on Sunday mornings? Don't assume you're missing out on anything by not living a life like that. Very few people do, and even fewer are happy with it. Don't worry about what's right for others. Think about what's right for you.

Of course, we all have blue periods. Maybe you go to a series of disappointing parties and feel down afterwards. Or maybe all the people you contact through the personal ads in the paper don't get back in touch with you. Maybe the last three new people you tried to talk to ended up being engaged. Maybe you need a rest.

That's no crime. In fact, enjoying your single life again may depend on your taking time out. Allow yourself to hibernate for a while before going back out there. We all have limits, and it's healthy to recognize them.

GREEN WITH ENVY

One trap some singles fall into is envying someone else who seems to be doing much better than they are. The truth may be that the person in question went through hell before being able to act so confidently or be so friendly. But even if that's not the case, and the issue is one of "natural talent," you must remember that that person is not you. You have positive points of your own, advantages you'll never be able to bring to the surface if you spend all your time comparing yourself to someone else.

Maybe your best friend answers five personal ads a week to stay motivated and psyched up, but when you even think about doing the same thing, you get exhausted. For you, making one call a week to a friend you haven't seen for a while, and meeting for a drink to trade notes and date candidates may be plenty of forward progress.

You might well decide to answer a personal ad or two when you feel you're ready. But that's for you to decide. Finding your own comfort level doesn't mean you never grow or change. It doesn't mean you never feel nervous, or never challenge yourself. All it means is that you do whatever you decide to do in a way that's consistent with who you are.

Mary Louise found that what used to work for her no longer worked. She once prided herself in going out four times a week and keeping in touch with lots of people she'd met on her evening adventures. But when she started a new job that pushed her to the limit, she didn't have the energy to go out on weeknights--and she didn't have time to call a lot of people she used to call during the day. But instead of going out anyway and arriving at work the next day feeling like a zombie, Mary Louise accepted that her approach to being single had to change--because her life had changed.

Everyone has a comfort level. A style. A speed. A way of acting and reacting that works best. Find yours and then own it. Once you do, don't let anyone else make you think you'd be better off being anyone other than you.

Chapter 26:
Get Out of
Your Rut

Not all dirty words have four letters. Some have three. So sharpen your pencil, turn down the stereo, and take the following quiz to see if you've fallen prey to one of the most common setbacks in the meeting-people game--getting into a ***.

The Rut Test

I eat the same thing for breakfast every day.

( ) always   ( ) mostly
( ) sometimes   ( ) never

Dinner at a Chinese restaurant means Moo Shu Pork for me.

( ) always   ( ) mostly
( ) sometimes   ( ) never

I'm very attached to my favorite TV shows, and never go out on the nights they're on.

( ) always   ( ) mostly
( ) sometimes   ( ) never

(For women:) After reading all those articles about how difficult it is to meet available men for women who are over 30, I'm so bummed out about the odds that I think, "Hey, why bother?"

( ) always   ( ) mostly
( ) sometimes   ( ) never

I exercise at the same time, in the same place, with the same routine, and in the same college tee-shirt, every time.

( ) always   ( ) mostly
( ) sometimes ( ) never

I call my mother (or best friend, or dial-a-horoscope) every day at the same time.

( ) always   ( ) mostly
( ) sometimes ( ) never

I read only books of a certain type (such as murder mysteries or work-related items).

( ) always   ( ) mostly
( ) sometimes ( ) never

(For men:) I don't date women who are over 30 or who are under 5' 7".

( ) always   ( ) mostly
( ) sometimes ( ) never

(For women:) I don't date men who don't have MBAs.

( ) always   ( ) mostly
( ) sometimes ( ) never

All my clothes are in shades of brown because that's the only color I look good in, and besides, having all brown clothes makes color coordinating easier.

( ) true   ( ) close to the mark
( ) rings a bell ( ) false

Did you check either of the first two responses for three or more questions? Did taking this test remind you of other ways in which you get the feeling that you're stuck doing the same things over and over? Does your rut extend from breakfast to infinity?

What you eat for breakfast is your business, but you should consider whether or not you want your future to be more exciting than two eggs over easy for the rest of your life. Read the following tips about breaking free from boring patterns--then *do something about it.*

A FEW ANTI-RUT TIPS

Wear color to make yourself stand out. No one's suggesting that you invest in a plastic fuschia dress, or that green neon tie you saw in the mail order catalog, but you should think seriously about adding some splash to your wardrobe. Wear something that will pull you out of the fashion woodwork--maybe a few sweaters in bright colors, or bold patterns, a pair of bright red suspenders, or any kind of stockings except taupe.

Accept that the quality of your life will not be compromised if you miss a special on HBO or an episode of thirtysomething. If you have problems with this one, buy a VCR.

Make a pact with yourself to get out of the house a certain number of nights a week--and stick to the plan. Map out the best way for you to accomplish this. Maybe one night you'll go out with a friend, and on another you'll go out alone. Maybe you'll meet a group of friends who'll expect you to be there each week. Or you might join a club with regular meetings. Devise a plan with a structure that will help you keep your commitment.

Alternate the time or route that you take to work. Do you take the same bus every day, and wait in line with the same people? Why not try taking an earlier or later bus? Even if you drive, you may encounter some new faces if you pull into the parking lot at a different time.

Don't eat lunch at the same place every day--and don't eat at your desk. Variety is the spice of life, remember? Besides, aren't you getting a little tired of the same blue plate specials day after day?

Get out of your chair! Unless, of course, the person sitting next to you is attractive, interesting, and single. Otherwise, move around at intermission or halftime. Go to the snack bar. Stretch your legs in the lobby. Check on the weather. No one will seek you out while you sit there passively, staring at your ticket. You have to stand up for yourself if you want to meet someone new at plays, sporting events, or other gatherings.

Alice joined a community theater group and decided to work as a stagehand, helping out with the lighting on a production of *Peer Gynt*. She didn't know a thing about lighting, but the others in the group taught her everything she needed to know. On rainy nights, when she would normally have said, "Why bother?", and would have spent the evening watching old movies alone and feeling sorry for herself, she found herself at rehearsal instead. And afterwards, she stops by a bar with a few of the actors and techies in the show. She found herself spending time with talented and creative people--people she never would have met if she hadn't become a vital part of the production.

Jim went to the same diner every day at the stroke of noon. The waitress no longer needed to ask what he wanted--his B.L.T. with extra mayo was ready when he walked through the door. But one afternoon he had a doctor's appointment, and decided to stop at the coffee shop near the medical building for a quick bite. He met Donna, who worked in a doctor's office as a receptionist. They ended up talking for forty-five minutes before they realized they were both late--he for his appointment, she for work. They were able to talk about the implications of their tardiness on their date that Saturday night.

Getting out of your rut isn't easy. Sometimes you won't feel like making the effort. Ruts become comfortable and safe places to stay, but they're deadly boring. If you wanted boring, you probably wouldn't have picked up this book. When the old, familiar routine seems tempting, remind yourself that you'll never know who you might have been or what else you might have done if you don't make the effort to climb out of your rut.

CHAPTER 27:
Look Around
Your Office

Consider for a moment how many hours you spend at work each year. You might very well put in more time at the office than you do anywhere else. When you think about it, using your workplace as a resource for your social life can make good sense.

This doesn't necessarily mean dating coworkers. But your colleagues may well have friends you can meet, and other departments or businesses in the building may have several potential mates for you. You have no idea what adorable but married secretary has a single sister--or what not-your-type manager has a very-your-type best friend.

Be open to meeting people from other companies who work in your building (or on your block). Start an interoffice softball league by inviting other businesses to participate. Ask someone exactly what his or her firm does, or if you can get an informal tour (because you've always been curious about what went on behind the scenes there). Don't neglect initiating conversation in the hallway or restroom--who knows who someone else might know?

Karen works in a big office; many people pass by her desk during the day. She put up a little plaque that read "Single and Looking." All sorts of people, of both sexes, started talking to Karen about being single. She not only got to know her office mates a little better, but she also greatly expanded her singles network.

Someone you work with might make a great friend--or even a good match for you. Times have changed since the office romance was considered taboo, and both dating rituals and friendship patterns have changed (especially with some people regularly working 60-hour weeks, or even longer). The office has now become a pool for meeting new people and making new friends, as well as a way to make a living.

A BAD EXCUSE

"I couldn't picture asking anyone from my office--man or woman--out for a beer after work. I spend enough time with those people already! Anyway, I don't think we'd have much in common besides the company, and who wants to talk shop?"

You might well be spending too much time at the office, but that doesn't mean you're spending too much time with the people in your office. If you take the time to get to know some of your coworkers *outside* work, you may be pleasantly surprised. Haven't you ever heard anyone say, "He's a completely different guy outside the office?" Don't jump to conclusions about someone based on what you know about how the person behaves at work--especially if the job in question makes a lot of demands on the person's time.

Everyone talks about the negative side of dating a coworker: you could end up competing for a promotion, or be accused of favoritism if you make business decisions that affect your office mate. But there is another side as well.

FIVE POSITIVE POINTS ABOUT
DATING SOMEONE AT THE OFFICE

When you work with someone all day, you'll get to know a tremendous amount about the person. You'll know about good moods, bad moods, tastes, habits. You'll have a much better idea of what the person is really like. Working together allows you to get to know someone gradually, usually without a lot of unrealistic expectations.

You'll learn about his or her background. Most people know if a coworker is involved, divorced, a single parent, a heartbreaker; you usually needn't wonder if the person is married, as you'll either know or be able to find out easily.

You probably dress well for work, so you'll each look polished, professional, and responsible when you see one another. What's more, doing a job you're good at allows you to show the person your confident, competent side.

You won't have to wonder if you'll ever see the person

again. Waiting by the phone may even become obsolete, because you know where the person is for at least eight hours of the day, and you know when you'll run into one another.

You have common interests. And built-in conversation starters, as well, inasmuch as you know the same people and are familiar with the workings of the same company.

ANOTHER BAD EXCUSE

"I'd never consider dating someone I work with because I'm afraid I could lose my job--or end up hating someone I still have to face every day."

Never say never! Some office romances do work. The nature of your jobs and the atmosphere of the company will, of course, make a difference. But if you ask yourself from the start how a potential relationship might affect your job and your career, you may find that you're able to steer around the potholes. You can set up ground rules from the beginning about how you want your relationship to be viewed (if at all) by other coworkers. Just remember that, even if you're open about your liaison, getting into hot clinches over the copy machine is not recommended.

Jeff felt very strongly that the office was not the place to talk about his personal life, let alone meet a mate. But after eating clams at a business lunch one day, he got a case of food poisoning that was so bad that his coworkers had to call an ambulance. One colleague, Cheryl, insisted on waiting with Jeff until help arrived; she asked if there was anyone she should call for him. He told her he wasn't married; Cheryl was surprised, and told him she hadn't known he was single--she was too, as it turned out. They spent the rest of the time waiting for the ambulance, talking about the ins and outs of single life. They even decided to talk some more over dinner (no clams, of course) when Jeff was feeling better.

You and your coworker/prospective mate may not always be working at the same place. If you lay the groundwork for a relationship while you are in the office together, you'll have a good chance to continue the relationship after one of you changes jobs . . . and perhaps even finalize things!

Katy and Steven met when Katy took a job in the office where Steven worked. She was attracted to Steven from the moment she saw him, but, because she was on the rebound from a bad breakup, she wasn't ready for a heavy-duty romance (especially with someone she'd have to face professionally every day). After three months of spending time getting to know Steve in a neutral atmosphere, Katy got an offer for a better job and left the company. After a while, she and Steven started dating. Less than a year after her departure from the original company, they were skiing together in Colorado, wearing sweaters they'd bought while vacationing in Greece. The next time they went to Greece, they got married.

CHAPTER 28:
Learn the Art
of Short Talk

Short talk means just that--a conversation that operates within a limited time frame. The beauty of short talk is that both parties are aware of this time frame from the outset, so there's less pressure, fewer reasons to be nervous, and a greater chance of "escalating" to a comfortable conversation.

Short talk works like this. Say you're at a singles party, and want to meet that dreamboat across the room--but you can't figure out how to get over there unnoticed (much less what you'll say when you get there). You rely on short talk. You go right up to the dreamboat and say, "Excuse me--can I talk to you for a few minutes? I'm trying to avoid someone." Isn't everyone at a singles party trying to avoid *someone*? If the person asks who, just answer that you'd rather not say.

LOW-RISK ENCOUNTERS

The key is that you've put a time limit on the conversation before it even begins. At the end of the ten minutes, you can thank the person and excuse yourself. You don't feel crushed if you didn't find a soul-mate, because you didn't take much of a risk. And you didn't waste the ten minutes because you used the time to practice initiating conversation.

That's something you'll notice about short talk the more you use it. You simply can't lose.

What's more, when you use this method, the person you approach will be less guarded; you won't be trying to monopolize time, so you'll be perceived as less of a threat. That means the person will actually listen to what you say instead of trying to figure out what you want. You've already said what you want--a few minutes of conversation, not company for the rest of your life, or even for the rest of the evening.

Louise uses short talk in bars. She looks at her watch, sighs, and then goes up to someone and asks if she can join him for a couple of minutes while she waits for a friend who's late. When the time is up, Louise says, "I can't believe she did this to me again. Next time I'll pick her up at her house or forget it." If the conversation has been going well, the man will usually suggest that Louise stay. If she'd rather not, she says that her friend lives nearby, and she might as well go see her while she's still mad enough to chew her out.

Gretel was sitting alone in a restaurant, and George decided he wanted to meet her. He went over to her table and said, "Excuse me. Do you mind if I sit here? That waitress is a friend of mine and all the other tables at her station are taken. I'm just going to have a quick ice cream fix and then leave. Would that be okay?" His companion muttered a barely audible assent, without even looking up from her book. George ordered a banana split, and when the dessert came, he asked the waitress (whom he did know casually) for two spoons. When she heard this, Gretel smiled, put her book down, and picked up a spoon.

If you have difficulty meeting people, think of short talk as an early, essential component of your "bag of tricks." These aren't the sort of tricks that fool other people into thinking you're someone you're not. This bag contains the tricks that are helpful when you want to put yourself out there and feel more confident in the process.

Every endeavor has a bag of tricks. Some pitchers rely on their curveballs when they get into tight spots. Some singers know that if they end a song with a long high note that's hit perfectly, they'll get applause even if the rest of the song was not perfect.

Your bag of tricks will contain "old reliables" you've memorized and can perform with ease--even when your stomach is filled with butterflies.

Short talk is an especially good trick you can use to initiate contact. This is because it lessens the chance that *both* of you will feel nervous and uncomfortable, and it reduces the likelihood that you'll feel rejected, since you have a gracious exit at your disposal if you need one.

CHAPTER 29:
Do Errands
in the
Evenings or
on Saturdays

If you're like most of us, you've probably never noticed much about your surroundings when you shop for food except whether or not chunky peanut butter is on sale. But food is more than something with which you must stock your cupboard.

It's a well-documented fact that every intelligent, attractive single person must eat. Every day. And even if they somehow manage to go out to dinner every night, your potential dates must still purchase light bulbs, toiletries, Drano, and other essentials, such as gourmet ice cream.

And when do these single people shop? Usually on the way home from work or on Saturdays. And here's another interesting fact: the people we're interested in may not want to make a big deal out of three bananas, a package of cocktail wieners, a carton of heavenly hash, and a quart of orange juice, but they do play by the same rules the rest of the world does. They have to wait in line. Think of the possibilities!

Once you think of buying groceries during the singles "rush hours" as an opportunity to strike up conversations with new people, an otherwise mundane chore can become an adventure. Even if chunky peanut butter *isn't* on sale after all.

PRACTICE MAKES PERFECT

Try practicing on the check-out clerk. Be friendly. Hand him or her your coupons before the bill is totalled to get on the checker's good side. If you like something the clerk is wearing or notice a flattering haircut, say so. After all, standing there all day ringing up mountains of groceries can get tedious. The clerk can probably use a kind word;

offering one will help you work your way up to making "aisle encounters" the next time you shop.

Now then. Suppose it *is* the next time. You're wheeling your cart down the aisle and you see someone interesting eyeing the frozen pizzas. Here's your plan.

Step One. Walk over to the frozen pizzas section yourself.

Step Two. Ask if the person has tried the brand he or she is pondering.

Step Three. Say you usually buy a competing brand, but you're not sure you're crazy about the choice and have been thinking about buying the brand the person is looking at.

Step Four. Try to engage in friendly conversation. If the plan didn't work, toss the new brand of frozen pizza into your cart, and be friendly to the clerk on the way out.

OTHER OPTIONS

The grocery store isn't the only place where singles run errands on evenings or weekends. Be open to meeting people dropping off dry cleaning, buying bandaids in the drugstore, or returning empty bottles. At the hardware store, ask someone's advice on what size picture hooks you need. At the flower stand, ask an interesting person what kind of flowers would best cheer up a sick friend.

Certainly you shouldn't consider these settings your only opportunities. You should consider, though, the advantages of extending your awareness of meeting places to include some non-traditional locales.

After all, you can meet people anywhere. Just review the places you met your last few significant others, and odds are you'll come up with a few settings you don't encounter every day. A snack stand at an outdoor concert or game. An adjoining open-air phone booth on a rainy day. In line to use the automatic teller.

There are countless stories of odd places people have found to begin relationships. Get out there and make one of your own.

Chapter 30:
Tell Yourself
You're Out
of Town

Brian spends a lot of time on the road for business. He gets lonely sometimes, so if he strikes up a conversation, Brian often invites the person to join him for dinner. He usually has at least one dinner guest for every few days he's away. While telling a friend about meeting a woman he took to dinner after accidentally spilling a club soda on her, Brian's friend looked at him and shook his head. "You have three times as many dates when you're 2,000 miles from home. Did you ever think about just dressing up, telling yourself you're on a business trip, and doing the same thing here in town?"

Mei Ching went to Jamaica with friends on a vacation. On the beach, she kept noticing an attractive man who was staying at their hotel; finally she decided to invite him to join her on a walk into town. Mei Ching couldn't stop laughing when she found out that the man (his name was Benjamin) lived twenty miles from her home town! She still kids him about having to go to the Caribbean to meet the boy next door.

Did you ever notice that you seem to have more fun when you're out of town? There are a number of reasons for this.

You know you won't run into anyone you know, specifically anyone who's likely to judge you or keep notes on you for the rest of your life and report you to The Authorities.

You know flirtation is harmless, and you're more willing to indulge in the fun.

You have a reason to be alone, and are less defensive

about your solo status.

Why can't you have the same type of fun at home? You can!

You can realize that even if you do run into someone you know, you're being charming and fun-loving, not lewd or bacchanalian. Besides, whoever you run into will probably be too busy running into new friends to record everything you do and say for future reference.

You can accept that flirtation is harmless, and realize that you might as well indulge.

You can allow yourself to be alone without having to have a reason, and thus be less defensive.

When people go on vacation, they go to have fun. Because of this, many vacationers are more assertive about meeting people than they would be otherwise. They've spent all this money and come all this way, and they're going to have some fun, dammit.

The thought of demanding as much from their daily lives as they do from their vacations never seems to cross their minds. They may as well have taken out a Limited License to Have Fun. "This certificate authorizes enjoyable activities only when you are further than 50 miles from your domicile; only when the nearest bathroom features a white paper 'sani-strip' over the toilet; and only when you feel confident that, if you leave your shoes outside the door, they will be cleaned rather than stolen."

Diane is a recruiter for a large corporation. She would never think of going to a bar alone when at home, but put her on a business trip and she'll hit a different night spot every evening. After all, Diane tells herself, what else is there to do? She doesn't have friends to call, laundry to do, or a living room to clean. She allows herself to be free and to act on that freedom. As a result, she's more relaxed, more open to meeting different types of people, and less uptight about the fact that she hasn't yet found the Love of Her Life. And if nothing happens, so what? She's going home in a few days.

What do you think would happen if Diane had that same attitude while she was at home?   What do you think would happen if *you* had that attitude?

CHAPTER 31:
Don't Be Afraid
of Failure

In his book *The Thanatos Syndrome*, novelist Walker Percy has provided us with perhaps the best definition of failure yet set to paper. "Failure," writes Percy, "is what people do 99 percent of the time."

As Percy points out, this stands in marked contrast to what people are *shown* doing most of the time. Think of a favorite film or television show. Things seem so perfect, and the conflicts and problems appear so manageable; everyone always has something interesting to say, and those witty, insightful, endearing comments always come at exactly the right moment. No one sneezes unexpectedly or spills something for no reason or delivers a line haltingly. The outcome of the episode is predetermined, and the ending always neat, intelligible, and on schedule.

Most of us have harbored secret thoughts at one time or another of entering that perfect world. We might ask, "Why can't my life be more like life is in (fill in your favorite show or film here)?"

We can't, of course. The ideal is a fantasy. And while there's nothing wrong with having fantasies, we need to appreciate the difference between a good fantasy and reality. It might help to see the dozens and dozens of takes from the "perfect world" that failed because the actors flubbed their lines, or a prop wouldn't work, or a light bulb burned out suddenly. (It might help even more to take a peek through the writers' first three dozen drafts of the script.)

So take heart. Maybe James Bond always gets the girl, but he's at a distinct disadvantage, because he isn't real. You are. If you find that you make silly mistakes and have minor imperfections, congratulations, you're a human being. So while the following list may not apply to Bond, it *does* apply to you.

THREE VITALLY IMPORTANT
POINTS FOR REAL PEOPLE

One. Life is filled with screwups.

Two. Even people who look like they never screw up, screw up.

Three. Most of our screwups aren't as bad as we think they are.

Suppose you wanted to learn how to ski. You'd expect to learn bit by bit, and you'd expect to fall. You wouldn't *want* to fall, but you would know you were going to do some falling on your way to being a good skier (and even after you got to be a *fabulous* skier). You'd expect to make some mistakes, and you would understand that making mistakes is part of the learning experience. The same is true of learning any other sport. In fact, the same is true of learning how to do just about anything, from algebra to mergers and acquisitions.

If you're not hard on yourself about the other things you attempt to learn in life, *don't be so hard on yourself about dating.* If you *are* hard on yourself about the other things you attempt to learn, don't be so hard on yourself, period.

Now that you're more willing to give yourself a break, you'll be open-minded enough to consider these next few VIPFRP items.

MORE VITALLY IMPORTANT
POINTS FOR REAL PEOPLE

Four. Not everyone you meet will be right for you; some of them will definitely be wrong for you.

Five. You can't possibly know if someone will be right or wrong for you before you try to meet and get to know the person.

Six. Meeting a "wrong"--or even several "wrongs" in a row--doesn't mean that *you* are wrong. All you're doing in these situations is increasing your chances of meeting a "right" on your next try.

Every time you allow someone else's rejection of you to make you feel like a failure, you're empowering that person. You're giving that person the power to decide for the universe and everyone in it whether you are terrific or trash. Do you really want to do this?

If you'd rather take back some of that power, you must

go into an encounter believing that you already are a terrific person, and that you'll stay a terrific person no matter what anyone else says or does.

In the workshop that formed the basis of this book, we use a tool called the "Dud of the Day," wherein people share their rejections--situations that they thought had marked them for life. Doing this proves that bad things *do* happen to good people all the time.

Many people tell some pretty awful stories, but only one gets to be the "Dud of the Day." The "losers" realize their stories aren't so bad (or unique) after all, and the "winner" gets so much support and empathy that he or she realizes that these situations do tend to get magnified as we live them, and aren't a true reflection of who we are in any fundamental sense.

Cheryl, a vivacious blonde, won "Dud of the Day" honors during a recent workshop. She told about meeting a wonderful man who was jogging in the park while she was walking her puppy. He stopped to chat, and the two really hit it off. The man told Cheryl that his office was planning a big formal party the following Saturday, and that he didn't have a date. He asked her to go; she said yes. That week, Cheryl spent a lot of money on her gown, and a lot of time fantasizing about her date--and the future. But on Friday, the man's secretary called and told Cheryl he wouldn't be going to the dance. He never called her again or answered any of her messages.

Alex took the prize a few nights later. He told about going to a Parents Without Partners dance, and noticing a woman in a bright red dress almost as soon as he walked in. Alex spent a whole hour working up the courage to ask this woman to dance. When he finally went over and asked her, she turned and walked away without even saying "no," let alone "thanks." She had completely ignored Alex's existence.

Usually, people keep rejection to themselves. This is because it's painful to be undervalued. People even think they deserved what happened to them, or that they caused it somehow. This is nonsense. You can't possibly be responsible for someone else's rudeness, insensitivity, bad taste, or cruelty.

Try to put what happened in perspective; stop investing others with the power to define you. Keep that privilege to yourself.

CHAPTER 32:
Learn How to
Take a Line

He's handing you a line." "That's the oldest line in the book." "I can't say that; it will sound like I'm giving her a line."

What is a line? Any opening sentence that doesn't reflect the real person delivering it because the words don't come from the heart.

That doesn't mean, however, that anyone who gives you a line is an insincere jerk.

To be sure, *some* of the people who give you lines will in fact be insincere jerks. But that's not the case with a great many people, and since you're now used to giving people a second chance (see Chapter Seven if you need to brush up on this), you can practice the principle with people who feed you lines.

Haven't you ever met someone so fabulous, so entrancing, so wonderful that you lost your ability to converse spontaneously, and ended up tossing off something stiff, something so stupid you wondered later if you'd heard it in some bad movie?

Did that make you a jerk?

Of course not. You were just nervous. We've all said things at one time or another that made us want to melt into the floor. The truth is that lots of people who deliver bad lines are just plain scared.

A BAD EXCUSE

"Scared of *me*? Nervous about talking to *me*? You've got to be kidding."

Anyone, repeat, anyone who seems interesting to someone else can easily make that someone else nervous--especially if the someone else makes the first move.

Lines come in many shapes and sizes, from the grating-yet-innocuous to the downright sleazy come-on. For this chapter, though, let's focus on the two that are most common: the brag and the cliche.

THE BRAG LINE

Joel showed up for the singles workshop several minutes late, and the round-the-room introductions were already underway. When it was his turn to introduce himself, he apologized for his tardiness, and explained, "I just came from breaking ground on my new house. I'm building it. Actually, my company is building it. I own my own company, and I own a lot of land, too. In fact, I meet a lot of people. I don't really know why I'm here."

Sylvia was discussing what she wanted out of her next relationship. "I do want to meet someone," she said, "but it has to be the right someone. I have a very cultured background. I went to a private school; I own my own home. Most men wouldn't fit into my social circles."

Both Joel and Sylvia reacted to their nervousness by trying to surround themselves with success, lest anyone see them as something less than successful or desirable. Joel and Sylvia aren't creeps; they weren't lying about owning a business or having gone to private school. They were just using those things to create a sense of self-esteem to compensate for a feeling of being rattled, being on the spot.

In short, they didn't want to look like losers, so they went overboard trying to look like winners. Their real selves were tongue-tied.

When you hear the brag line, don't look for the exit. Go fishing. Try to hook the real person. You may be surprised at what you find just below the surface.

THE CLICHE LINE

Rob says that when he gets nervous around a woman, things like "Haven't I seen you someplace before?" and "Do you come here often?" fly out of his mouth before he can stop himself. He knows better, of course. He tries to say things that are witty and charming, but the cliches somehow pop out on their own.

Some people use up all their good sense when they make the effort to walk over and start a conversation. Give them credit for trying. They may need your help to get over the cliche hurdle; by all means, help.

The secret is to give the person a chance to relax long enough to say something real. Maybe the woman who asked your astrological sign had a hard day at the office. Maybe the guy who asks what a wonderful woman like you is doing in a place like this just came out of a long relationship, and isn't up to speed on initiating conversation with women. Maybe it's all these people could do to go to a new place by themselves and begin to socialize. And maybe one of them is someone you could really go for after all.

But if you take the opening line at face value, and move on--if you don't learn to take a line--you'll never know.

CHAPTER 33:
Throw a
"Non-Signficant Other" Party

David and Marina have been best friends for years. They know everything about each other. David is talented, attractive, witty, intelligent, and he has a great job. He also makes a mean chicken salad with green grapes. Marina would trust David with anything. She loves him dearly, *but she has never once dated him.* They just don't have the right chemistry together. Marina has seen other women go ga-ga for David, some of whom *did* have the right chemistry. And some of David's friends, of course, might have chemistry that works with Marina.

Why not find five, ten, or twenty other women who have a David in their lives (or a combination of women and men who have similar friends) and throw a party? Not only might you find someone wonderful for your good friends, but one of their non-significant others might be wonderful for you.

Another way to do this is to start with a group of five and have each of you ask five other "couples." That way, you'll also have the chance to meet interesting same-sex friends of friends, too.

Fred first heard about a "Bring Your Non-Significant Other" party when he read a personal ad. Fred went--along with lots of other people who responded to the ad--and he had a blast. He said the party was one of the most original get-togethers he'd ever attended, and he met several new people he planned to see.

When you're making out the guest list, think of people at your office, single parents of your kids' friends, and cousins and other relatives you can stand being in the same room with for more than an hour. How about people you know from the gym or the bowling league or the local ski club? Don't discount talking about the party with married friends-- they might well know other singles who would be interested.

Here's the best part. These parties are virtually jerk-proof! Each guest has vouched for his or her "date," leading to a certain amount of pre-screening. Try to find a bar that can make the same claim!

An interesting variation: if you have mostly married friends, each of whom never tires of telling you about friends of theirs you might like to meet, throw a party of your own--with the "admission price" being a single person of the opposite sex! In the right setting, and with the right people, you can keep yourself in dates for weeks at a time.

CHAPTER 34:
For Women Only

Rhonda has gotten twenty years of mileage out of four names. She had a sports-crazed beau a few years back, and he insisted she memorize the names of the Fearsome Foursome on the 1967 Los Angeles Rams: Deacon Jones, Rosey Grier, Roger Brown, and Merlin Olsen. She'd recite them casually at parties and stun her beau's buddies. Her boyfriend is ancient history, but she can still stand out from the crowd by injecting the Foursome into a conversation with an interesting man, then smiling and ordering them both another drink.

Well, these things do have their limits. No one's suggesting you learn reams of batting averages for the sole purpose of performing parlor tricks at someone else's whim. (We all remember the movie *Diner*, right?) Rhonda's story does illustrate an important point, though. A little bit of knowledge when it comes to football (or baseball, or basketball) can go a long way with sports fans. And whole lot of guys out there are sports fans.

Most men love at least one sport--and, just as important, love to talk about that sport. They may be nervous striking up a conversation with women, but if the conversation turns to Roger Clemens, they loosen right up.

So why not learn just a little bit about sports to make the conversation flow more easily at critical moments? You don't have to memorize the names, positions, and jersey numbers of all the players in the N.F.L.; a basic understanding of how the game is played and scored will do.

One way to use such information to your advantage is to go to a sports bar (or a bar that often features a sporting event on television). If you go on a night when a championship game is scheduled, get there early, because you'll be sharing the bar with lots of guys who have broken televisions, who are in town on business, or who just like to watch these things in a friendly setting.

It adds up to a lot of men, all of them interested in sports. And sports is something you can talk about!

Use the opportunity. Practice initiating and carrying on conversations that you know will interest the person you're talking to.   (In fact, if you play your cards right, you'll be able to talk about the game without really knowing that much about the sport!)

Judy went to a sports bar on the night of a big basketball game and sat quietly on her stool, watching the screen. Men were milling around everywhere. After the home team made a particularly difficult basket, Judy turned to the man seated next to her and said, "Nice shot."   Even Judy, who knew virtually nothing about basketball, knew a nice shot when she saw one. The fellow was very nice, and though he turned out to be married, he did tell her quite a lot about basketball. She used the information on subsequent (and steadily more confident) trips.

Be prepared for things to get a little rowdy, and leave if the scene starts to get out of hand. But don't be scared too easily.

Of course, it's also possible that things will be anything *but* rowdy. Many women complain that televised sporting events (particularly baseball games) are boring. You know what?   They're often right. Lots of games are boring. Some are over almost before they begin. Then what have you got? A whole room full of men watching a boring ballgame, with no plans for the rest of the evening. It's a shame, isn't it?

A WORD TO THE WISE
Warning: You will be, you must remember, in a bar. Lots of men will be drinking if their team isn't doing well. (In fact, lots of men will be drinking if their team *is* doing well.)   If someone gets frisky, tell him you'll give him a punch in the nose that will send him straight to Cooperstown. If that doesn't work, call over the bartender. If it *was* the bartender, find another bar.

Even if you're not crazy about bars, you can still use the sports principle to your advantage. A Boston woman we know wears a Red Sox cap to the beach, and finds that men are always stopping to comment on her headgear. In the fall, she wears a Patriots sweatshirt. And, of course, there's always . . .

THE SPORTS PARTY

You might consider throwing your own Super Bowl (or World Series, or NCAA Finals, or whatever) party: you provide the chicken wings and pizza, the guests bring the beer. Set up the room so that the screen can be seen from all angles, and make it clear to all comers that the party begins after the game, because the game itself will be treated like a religious service. (And mean it!)

Don't constantly pass the food around, or ask if anyone wants something else to drink. The rules for being a good hostess change in this setting. The guys will know, as if by some strange, primitive instinct, where the chicken wings and beer are--and you don't have to worry about them being shy about grabbing what refreshments they want. They won't be thinking about being polite; they'll be thinking about whether or not their team has time to make a field goal before halftime.

More revisions of standard etiquette: late arrivals go unintroduced until the Words From Our Sponsors at sports parties. No one will be listening to the introductions anyway, so don't even waste your time trying. Just hand the latecomer something to drink and vaguely shoo him or her into the television room.

Do not give in to the temptation to chat with other women present. You will instantly lose whatever credibility you've built up to this point. Stare intently at the screen. Try to figure out what's happening. If your best friend insists on flirting with that cute guy over in the corner, shoot her a look that says you're willing to show her what clipping really means.

PLACES TO MEET MEN THAT HAVE
NOTHING TO DO WITH SPORTS

Okay. So you hate spectator sports. You have other options. As we've noted elsewhere, one of the best is to go to a jazz club. Jazz musicians (as well as jazz enthusiasts) are predominantly male. Consequently, jazz clubs pack in more men than women. Lots more.

Forget the negative stereotypes normally associated with

musicians. Full-time musicians are educated, creative businessmen, many of whom earn excellent incomes by just playing, or by combining performing with teaching and recording. Part-time musicians may be anything from mechanics to CEOs during the day.

So go to everything from jam sessions to bona fide concerts, and the odds are that you'll find yourself with a man on either side of you at the bar.

If you don't meet anyone, at least you'll hear some great music--our country's original art form, to be exact. Don't sing the blues. Check out the jazz.

CHAPTER 35:
For Men Only

What's a guaranteed way to take a woman in your arms and make her feel wonderful? (Hint: Think of Gene Kelly, Fred Astaire, Gregory Hines, and Mikhail Baryshnikov.)

Women love to dance. When a woman daydreams, she often imagines herself in the center of a dance floor with nimble men who can salsa, waltz, samba, and maybe even do the froog. It's no coincidence that Cinderella meets her prince at the ball. Dance is a metaphor for intimacy and passion. (Ask anyone who's ever done the tango.)

Now. What do you do with this piece of knowledge? Take dancing lessons! Jazz dance, ballroom dance, swing dance, disco dance, modern dance--any kind. The nicest part of this is that the class you take will be filled with women who love to dance (or would love to know how). You don't have to be perfect. You don't even have to be good. You just have try.

The mere willingness to get out there on the floor will instantly set you apart from the crowd. If it's a challenge, so what? You like challenges, don't you? (Besides, most women don't exactly threaten Ginger Rogers, either.)

Think about this for a moment. The women in your class will probably need to practice. They might even want to practice in between classes with a nice guy like you.

Rick is a computer programmer who spends his days at work in a tiny cubicle writing programs. He works long hours and is a little shy. He hadn't been on a dance floor since ninth grade when he joined a group called the Rugcutters for a few months. Now Rick goes out to dance with his group every Thursday; they meet socially two nights a week, as well. Seven women are in the group; Rick dances with them all. To his delight, other women see him on the floor and come over to ask him to dance. He's in great demand, and he's loving every minute of it.

It bears repeating. You don't have to be graceful, or gorgeous, or even a particularly good dancer. All you have to be is willing.

ANOTHER OPTION

Take an aerobics class. Out of a class of 30 people, how many do you think are women? Put it this way: the odds are in your favor. And while you're meeting women, you'll be getting fit.

***

Joe is a nice guy; a little chubby, great company, and eager to try new ideas. He was interested in taking an aerobics class, but he worried that his "full figure" wouldn't win him any prizes with the women in the class. In his worst moments, he even feared they'd laugh at him. But he decided to go for it anyway. And guess what happened? All the women were wonderful to him. They encouraged him, and said it was about time someone was man enough to take an aerobics class. Now, Joe's looking much slimmer, and getting lots of attention from two dozen women in leotards. You could say he's in pretty good shape.

CHAPTER 36:
Take a Class

C lass is no longer something you devise ways to skip. Adult learning centers, the YMCA and YWCA, and even colleges and high schools offer evening and weekend classes and workshops for adults on everything from wine tasting to learning how to buy your first condominium.

No matter what the subject, each class will not only teach you something new, but also give you the chance to meet people who are guaranteed to have at least one thing in common with you--your interest in the class.

Look for ads and announcements about these classes, which may be one-shot lectures or longer series, in the local paper, alternative periodicals like *Rolling Stone*, singles publications, cable television and community bulletin boards, laundromats, and campuses.

Some of the topics will be quite serious (financial planning, for instance); others be more non-traditional (exploration of "past lives"). Some teach hands-on skills (boating safety or CPR); others will be more opportunity-oriented (how to be an airline courier and travel for free). Some of the "classes" will actually be trips--hikes, hot air balloon rides, or white water rafting. Think about any subject or activity you'd like to learn more about, and you'll find a class somewhere that covers it.

The opportunities seem endless; a recent scan through some of the course offerings of a major adult education program included: resume writing; massage; modern dance; basic computer programming; scuba diving; modeling; writing mystery novels; losing your Brooklyn accent; overcoming fear of flying; assertiveness training; shopping for bargains . . . the list goes on and on. The only reason you won't find a course that's right for you is that you didn't try in the first place.

Paula took a class in job hunting skills; she felt trapped in the secretarial position she'd been in for two years. She needed some advice on how to get into something better. Meeting a lover was not at the top of her list, but Peter sat down next to her on the first evening of the course she selected. Peter and Paula, it turned out, had a lot in common; they exchanged phone numbers and called each other for support quite a bit over the next few months as they each embarked on the job search. The contact kept them motivated; each knew there'd be a reckoning with the other person if he or she started to slack off. They're still in touch, even though they both found new jobs they like.

A BAD EXCUSE

"There are too many of these classes that sound interesting. I couldn't possibly pick just one."

So pick two. Or four. Or a dozen. Who says you have to stop at one? The only limits are your time and imagination. (Most courses are surprisingly affordable, so money usually isn't a problem.)

Consider choosing a class that's likely to attract more people of the opposite gender than your own. For example, more women than men may take a self-defense class, and more men than women may be in a course on how to repair cars. Ask the registration personnel for help in selecting the right course.

Even if you don't meet anyone special in the class, you'll have a great topic for conversation the next time you need one. Knowing about something someone doesn't expect you to know about (or even be interested in) sets you apart from the crowd. If nothing else, you'll be remembered.

Some of these classes, especially those in the "personal growth" category, are specifically geared toward singles. Some of the course titles will tip you off right away. ("How To Be Married a Year From Now" is a good example.) Taking one of these classes is a really great way to see what singles live in your community, and to make new friends as well. Use these classes to broaden your singles network and find out what other singles are doing--where they're going to meet new men and women. If you use these classes only for mate searching, you'll pass over a lot of interesting folks.

You might also want to consider taking a traditional textbooks-lecture-and-notes evening class at a local college.

Think about it. Isn't there some subject you used to love, a subject you put aside because you thought you couldn't spend time on learning anymore?   Do you want to bone up on Proust?   Has a decade passed since you wrote your last poem?   Have you always wanted to speak Greek?   You may be amazed at the things you can awaken within yourself by reopening a chapter you once loved, but never got around to finishing.

Marie is a lawyer who loved doing watercolors as a girl, but didn't pursue art after high school--she never thought she was good enough. After being inspired by an exhibit at the art museum, Marie decided to take a weekend class in watercolors. She found that all the old excitement returned; she was able to express things she'd never been able to, and in a way she hadn't tried in years. Marie's interest and talent were so genuine that the instructor took a real interest in her work; they began meeting after class to talk about art. Six months later, after the class had concluded, they were still getting together on the weekends to critique each other's projects.

Go ahead. Sign up for "Waist Whittling," "How to Speak French Like a Native," or "How to Make a Million Bucks and Retire Before You're 40."   (Who cares if you're 42?) The important thing is that you're *putting yourself out there.*

CHAPTER 37:
Attend Weddings, Reunions, Alumni Functions, and Family Gatherings

Maybe your mother lectures you a lot about why you're not married yet. Maybe your father has hated every potential mate you've ever brought home. Even so, chances are good that no one cares more about your happiness than your family. Take advantage of that concern, no matter how misguided it may appear to you at times, and consider your family as a resource.

That means showing up at family functions, despite your low tolerance for Aunt Sophie's stories, Uncle Henry's nosy questions, and your sister's screaming kids.

Donna used to hate going home for holidays. Every year, her huge family held a July 4th barbecue, and she was expected to attend, no matter what. She usually bypassed something more interesting that a friend was doing, gritted her teeth, and endured the afternoon--until last year. After taking a workshop for singles, she decided to try using her family as a resource. She ended up talking to a cousin who was about ten years out of her age range, and telling him that she was trying to meet someone. He said he was doing the same thing, and asked Donna if she wanted to go to a local pub to compare notes--outside of Grandma Justine's earshot. They did just that, and surprised themselves with how much they had in common. They agreed to stay on the lookout for each other.

Weddings are another good family function to show up for, especially since they usually include people who aren't related to either family. Lots of couples meet at someone else's wedding, and if you think about it, that's not surprising. Everyone is dressed to the nines. The atmosphere is relaxed and celebratory. There's plenty of food and drink. And no one feels the pressure to perform that's so common in "pick-up" situations.

Take advantage of all those factors; have a good time and see who else is doing the same. Ask someone twenty years older than you to dance. Ask someone twenty years *younger* than you to dance. The message will get across: you're a fun, friendly, outgoing person. You're not just a friend of the bride's sitting impassively at Table Eleven.

Mae had kept in touch with her best friend from junior high, Prudence, for almost twenty years. Prudence invited Mae to her wedding, and mentioned something about an Uncle Matthew flying in from California to attend. Mae had an image in mind of Uncle Matthew based on her own uncles--middle-aged men who worked too hard and smoked cigars she couldn't stand. She did a classic double take when the real Uncle Matthew, who looked like the male lead on a soap opera, showed up. Normally she would have been nervous approaching someone she didn't know, but now . . . maybe it was the champagne, or the band, or the terrific dress she was wearing, but something made her walk right up to him as "Blue Eyes" floated over the dance hall, take his arm, gesture toward his eyes, and say "I don't think they make them any bluer than that."   He smiled and accompanied her to the dance floor.

Next to consider are high school and college reunions, even though you only get one shot every five years. Don't judge people ahead of time. The detention king who bucked authority may have used his fire to write a great novel--and become a great catch. Many divorced people attend these functions, and even married couples have friends and relatives you might be interested to hear about.

If you're afraid you'll look like a failure asking old

schoolmates if they know anyone you might like to meet, don't act like a failure. Say you're single, you've been dating a lot, and you'd like to date some more. You haven't found the right match yet, but you sure have been trying. Any chance they know anyone?

Leon was surprised at how his twentieth reunion went. Lots of the people who attended were classmates he didn't even remember. Many of the singles came in groups; Leon found plenty of people he enjoyed talking to who were also available. The biggest surprise was that his main high school crush, Priscilla, who had dated the quarterback for three years, was now traveling solo--she told Leon she'd always thought he was a doll.

Here's a variation to consider. Join your college alumni association (and its local chapter if you live in another town), and work on the committee that schedules non-reunion alumni events. If no such committee exists, start one!

Even if you don't have big family gatherings, and you hate school reunions because people always offer backhanded compliments like "You're looking *so* much better these days," keep an open mind. People from your past can be an invaluable resource.

Jim lives in Manhattan. His mother called from Ohio to let him know that a woman she met in the supermarket had a daughter named Denise, who had just moved to Manhattan. His mother remembered how hard not knowing anyone in the city had been for him in the beginning, so she asked him to call Denise and see if she needed anything. (What she didn't say was that she'd promised Denise's mother that Jim would call.)   At first, Jim was annoyed; he remembered the time his mother promised a neighbor that Jim would mow the lawn next door for the seven weeks the neighbor was on vacation--free of charge. It was typical. He called Denise anyway, though, and never regretted it . . . not even when he hurt his back carrying Denise's new bureau up four flights of stairs.

CHAPTER 38: Join a Professional Organization

Rita, a graphic designer, was dating a man she liked, but the relationship didn't seem to be leading to anything permanent. She wanted a big family, and her boyfriend didn't seem to want marriage or kids. Around the same time, she decided to take a chance in her career, and went freelance. To make more contacts, she also decided to join a graphic artists' guild in her area. She liked the guild so much that she got more and more involved, and ended up being a co-chair for an important committee. Jack was also on that committee. Rita and Jack hit it off well, but never dated, because of Rita's relationship with her boyfriend. They got to know each other quite well as friends and coworkers; eventually, Rita's love interest fizzled, but her relationship with Jack sizzled.

Does your profession have a guild or association? A networking group? If so, get involved. Go to the meetings and the happy hours. Join a committee. Get to know the other members; see what happens.

TWO BAD EXCUSES
"My profession doesn't have a group like that."
"My profession does have a group like that, but I can't stand the people in it."
So join something else!

Allen is a senior partner in a big-city law firm; his long hours on the job make having a social life difficult. He's also shy, and initiating conversation doesn't come easily to him. But since his profession has made him a rather wealthy man, he decided he wanted to give something back to the community. He joined an organization for executives eager to contribute their efforts to charitable causes. He was placed on a brainstorming committee with Deena, a public relations specialist. After a while, he asked her out to dinner to discuss an upcoming project. A year later, they moved in together.

There are lots of other options. Do volunteer work for a charity or non-profit organization (public television pledge drives are a great place to start). Get involved in activities with your church or synagogue, or attend meetings of a self-help group if that's appropriate or necessary for you.

Of course, you shouldn't work for a charity or join Alcoholics Anonymous for the sole purpose of finding a mate, but thousands of couples end up meeting this way. Those in volunteer positions find they have similar interests and values; those who meet in self-help settings often use the high levels of group trust in such environments as a welcome advantage.

However you proceed, you'll find that by doing something good for your soul and your spirit, you'll be in a healthier frame of mind for meeting people and developing relationships.

CHAPTER 39:
Join a Health Club or Take Up a Sport

Don't think of working out or playing a sport as merely physical exercise. Think of these activities as social exercises as well. When you take the jumping jacks out of your living room and into the aerobics room, you'll get thinner, and healthier, and muscles that ache . . . but you'll also get new friends to complain to about the pain (as well as the gain). These are people who can teach you new routines, people who can inspire you to keep going, people to whom you can say, "Let's forget about these rowing machines and get a beer."

Health clubs are one place to start. There, you can take lessons in a new sport, sign up for a racquetball tournament (and meet a new partner), ask someone to show you how to use the weight machines or the treadmill, and so on.

Think about what activities at the club usually attract people of the opposite sex. Sign up for those activities. Men are often outnumbered at aerobics classes, for instance; women may find more men than women on the weight machines.

And here's a nice little bonus: everyone you meet at a health club is either in good shape or trying to get there.

Vary the times you go to the club--at lunch, after work, on the weekends. You'll meet different people at different times, and end up running into more people than you would if you went at one specific time.

Warning: Don't interrupt anyone doing a routine or in the middle of repetitive exercise. Wait until the person is done. Otherwise, you could break the person's concentration, which will not score you any points and might even get someone angry.

A BAD EXCUSE

"Health clubs are too expensive."

Join one that isn't as high-priced, such as the YMCA or YWCA. If you can't even afford that, maybe you can afford one class. And there's always jogging.

Linda was in the mood for a greater challenge than jazz dance class when she signed up for a boot camp training program at the Y. The class was filled with exactly the type of people you'd expect to find--men eager to get into top shape. On the first day, she noticed a man laughing at her as she started her push-ups. Linda ignored him, but later found out his name was Major. Later, when she was doing flexibility exercises, Major commented on how flexible Linda was for her age (42). Some time later, Linda asked the instructor Major's age. At the next session, she approached Major as he was exercising and said with a wry smile, "You're pretty flexible for a guy of 55!"

You might also consider taking up golf or tennis. You can join a country club, or just take lessons there--or take classes from your community recreation department. Then there's always the option of going out to a driving range on a balmy summer evening.

If you don't think you want to learn golf or tennis, think about volunteering to help with a tournament.

Sandy works for a large corporation that has its own golf tournament for clients and people in the industry. Although she had no interest in the sport, Sandy was asked to join the welcoming committee. Her job was to register players, then meet-and-greet at the eighteenth hole. Although Sandy didn't think working at the tournament would be much fun, she had a wonderful time. She couldn't believe how friendly everyone was, and she found herself following the progress of the players she found most interesting.

If you do decide to join a country club or gym, research the matter as seriously and as thoroughly as you would if you were buying a car. Ask what extra membership benefits there are, such as group trips, parties, or dances. Ask for a tour (this will also give you an idea of what crazy outfits are hip to sweat in these days). Ask if the club offers trial memberships or visits, and if it doesn't, take a class or two to get a feel for what membership would be like.

Ask others you meet there if they think their memberships are worthwhile--and what they get out of them.

If you decide not to join one of these places, consider other options. Take scuba diving lessons, join a swimming club, drag your skis or skates out of the closet, go bowling on Saturday nights, or team up with a community jogging group.

Annie warms up before running in the park on the weekends, and she recently noticed another jogger warming up about the same time but in a different spot. Annie has decided to change the place where she usually warms up so she can try to meet this man. She figures that if her efforts fail, she'll just stretch until she's warmed up and then literally run off into the sunset.

Part of the reason joining a health club or taking up a sport works is that it gets you out of the house and allows you to concentrate on something other than how what you're wearing looks or what clever thing you can say. Not that you won't sweat just as hard coming up with the perfect witty comment to make to the woman you just met in tennis class as you do in the class itself, but meeting others won't be your exclusive focus, and that fact should take some pressure off.

CHAPTER 40: Spend Time in Art Galleries and Museums

Never pass up a party--especially a free party full of interesting and creative people. Many such affairs are sponsored by art galleries and museums that are opening new shows or exhibits. Crowded parties make good publicity, and publicity is what the museums are after. In short, they want your body. (Obviously, they know something the rest of the world would do well to learn.)

Listings in the paper or city magazines frequently announce these opportunities; once you're there, be sure to get on the mailing list for future invitations. (If you're at a gallery, you may be able to get on two mailing lists. Sometimes artists have their own lists to inform their followers of new openings and shows.)

Walk around. Look at the show. Try to meet everyone: the artists who created the paintings or sculptures; the people who put the museum exhibit together; fellow gallerygoers.

Put in some time around the hors d'ouevres table or the bar. Everyone who goes to these things will end up at one or the other location eventually.

A BAD EXCUSE

"I hate the refreshments at those things--bad wine and hard little squares of cheese."

Who said you're only there for the beer? Keep in mind that every social setting carries with it certain disadvantages. Grit your teeth and plow ahead in the name of love.

Judy is on the mailing list of every gallery in her city. Openings are a ritual for her. She treats each announcement card she gets in the mail as a party invitation. Sometimes she gets all dressed up, pretending she's rich enough to be a potential buyer; sometimes she dresses *down*, as though she were a bohemian artiste type. She walks through the entire show once, silently sizing up the room and the people. Then she goes through again and compliments the artists whose work she likes, asking questions about the most interesting pieces. Sometimes she ends up with a group of people who invite her out for drinks; sometimes she simply goes home after the first hour or so. But she's had many more good times than boring times.

If you miss the special opening show of a museum (maybe because only members were invited), go see the exhibit as soon as it is open to the public. Special shows usually attract long lines. They're a perfect opportunity to meet other people who are standing around with nothing to do. And you'll have a built-in conversation piece: what you're waiting to see (as well as what other exhibits you've seen there recently). You never have to worry about being in a museum and having nothing to talk about, though you should wear or bring your own conversation piece to maximize your chances.

If you don't want to go alone--bring a friend along to act as your "icebreaker"!

Patty is an intelligent and interesting woman who likes to have a little help getting started with new people. She goes out with her friend Leslie, who can carry on a conversation with anyone from a prime minister to a beagle. Leslie starts the conversations and gets them going; when Patty gets more comfortable, she pipes in with her opinion. Going out with Leslie is a big asset for Patty.

Don't forget that museum cafeterias and dining rooms are great places to meet people. So are the front steps where folks sit, read, and people-watch in warm weather. Try going at different times--you may find it easier to meet others during the off hours, when the crowds are thinner.

While you're spending so much time at the museum, consider becoming a member; you'll be invited to special events as well as free films and lectures. Alternatively, you might volunteer to work at an exhibit.

Art galleries and museums aren't the only places that have openings. Be on the lookout for similar events at theatres, upscale restaurants and hotels, or other establishments. Don't assume that you can't go if the event is "private." Use some ingenuity!

Sandy walked by a fancy clothing store on her way home from work one night, and noticed that the store was having what appeared to be a private but informal party. She snuck in, smiled at everyone, and mingled. The people she met would tell Sandy who they knew--and ask who she knew. "Oh, I just crashed," she would reply, getting a big laugh each time. No one believed her. But they all liked her.

Artie found out that a large hotel that had just been built was having a formal opening party. He rented a tux and went. Even though the hotel issued name tags, Artie knew that no man goes to the expense of renting a tux to turn around and put a tacky nametag on it. On his arrival, he saw that he was right; all the guests had quickly removed their tags. Artie smiled as he entered, exchanged numbers with a few enchanting women, and had a wonderful time.

CHAPTER 41:
Take a Fabulous Vacation (Especially If It's Designed for Singles)

There's more to singles vacations than Club Med. Call a travel agent and ask what he or she has available that's especially designed for singles, including some of the more popular singles-only cruises. Keep an eye out for ads in the travel section of your newspaper and other periodicals (especially singles publications).

If you're still in college, look on your university bulletin board; if you're long out of school, call an adult education center that offers offbeat or unusual opportunities, in addition to more traditional classes.

You might even join a service that matches you up with other singles looking for traveling companions. The information is out there, and when you start looking for it, you'll have more to choose from than you ever imagined.

If you're hesitant about a particular tour, try to find someone who's gone on it before and ask about it. If you don't know anyone who has, call the reservations number and see if you can get some references.

You have a lot of options for lots of different kinds of vacations. If you're the shy type, think about a more structured trip--one that plans group activities that will make it easy for you to keep busy and interact with other people. If you hate having your days planned and don't need any help mingling, less structured trips are your answer.

Even if you don't meet anyone, a vacation will relax you and put you in a more positive frame of mind for meeting others once you return. Don't underestimate the importance of this change in outlook. Bring that relaxed, open feeling home with you so you can reconstruct it when you need it, knowing that the "real" you is waiting inside to be summoned.

Note: If you can get some brochures for singles trips, think about using them as a conversation piece in conjunction with other ideas in this book.

For those of you running to pack, skip the rest of this chapter. For those of you *not* running to pack, the rest of this chapter is especially for you.

THE FIRST BAD EXCUSE

"I can't afford a vacation."

Investigate the options before you dismiss the idea out of hand. Lots of singles vacations are package deals at extremely attractive prices, especially if you travel in the off season.

THE SECOND BAD EXCUSE

"Why bother? If I meet someone interesting, odds are the person will live far away from me."

Plenty of relationships survive long distances. Besides, maybe the person is thinking of moving anyway. Maybe *you're* thinking of moving anyway. You might find someone who likes to travel, and could visit you often enough to make it all worthwhile. You'd travel for someone who seemed perfect in everything but geographical location, wouldn't you? Well, wouldn't you?

THE THIRD BAD EXCUSE

"All the singles trips are to tropical places, and I hate hot weather."

So go skiing instead. Don't say you don't know how to ski; that's what ski instructors and ski classes are for. Even if you *can* ski, why pass up the chance to spend a few hours with five or ten other skiers? Even if you're not attracted to any of them, you might get an invitation to a party where you could meet someone who does attract your attention.

If you have absolutely no interest in skiing whatsoever, go anyway and don't ski. Every major ski resort offers plenty of other options for all the non-skiers who come with their skiing friends. You can snowmobile, go cross country skiing, dog sledding, sleigh riding, shopping, or just sit in the hot tub. There are worse fates in life.

If skiing doesn't do much for you, but you like the idea of a sports camp, how about tennis camp? Most sports have camps that both teach beginners and sharpen the skills of the experts. And you're guaranteed to have something in common with the other singles you meet. Behold the instant conversation piece!

THE FOURTH BAD EXCUSE

"No one wants to go with me, and I could never go away by myself."

Have you been reading this book, or just thumbing through it during commercials?

THE FIFTH BAD EXCUSE

"I hate the idea of a vacation just for singles--it seems too much like a meat market."

Write your own ticket. Take any kind of vacation you want. Do what makes you feel comfortable. But go. And wherever you end up, keep on the lookout for interesting people to meet.

GETTING OUT AND INTO IT

Although they're not specifically set up to be singles vacations, groups like the Sierra Club, Earthwatch, and the Appalachian Mountain Club often sponsor trips that attract singles. Adventure travel of any kind is an excellent opportunity to meet others, and is the perfect answer to those who don't want to lie on a beach for two weeks. If there's a particular activity you enjoy (deep sea fishing, camping, nature photography), chances are someone, somewhere has arranged a group trip around your interest.

While you're dreaming about the new people you'll meet on your fabulous vacation, don't overlook the new people you'll meet *on your way* to said fabulous vacation. Talk to people standing next to you in line at airports, buses, and trains--and to any interesting-looking people who sit next to you once you're on board. Not to mention the cutie sitting six rows away.

And don't forget to pack your conversation piece!

CHAPTER 42:
Learn How
to Flirt

Martha went alone to Paris on a vacation, hoping for a little adventure and a major exotic romance. At a classic Parisian nightspot, she eyed an interesting man at the other side of the bar--and he eyed her back. Martha took a cigarette from her case, wrote her name and hotel phone number on the side, lit the cigarette and walked toward the man. She placed it in his ashtray and walked out. He got the message and called the next day.

Let's face it. Flirting can be fun. It's a flight of verbal (or, occasionally, non-verbal) fancy. To flirt is to give in to your childlike self and act spontaneously. The episode can last for a few seconds (as long as it takes to wink), or it can turn into weeks, months, or even years of trading witty quips.

In any form, flirting is best accomplished when you're feeling confident. Whether you're passing your number to someone in a smoky bar, or sending someone flowers with a poem, you can't do it well unless you're feeling good about yourself. The day you reach your weight goal, the day you got the account you've been sweating over for the last six months, the day you get a great new hairstyling--these are bound to be good days for you in more ways than one.

WHERE DO YOU START?

If confidence in social settings isn't exactly your strong suit, you might find it easier to start with the zipless flirt. That's a long-distance, passing-on-life's-highway interjection to an Intriguing Stranger. You may have encountered the zipless flirt yourself on occasion. In its most basic form, it's the "Hiya, gorgeous!" from someone who's just far enough away to make it interesting, rather than offensive. Truck drivers are fond of the maneuver.

The zipless flirt is popular because it involves a limited

display of courage and very little risk. Don't be crude; you're trying to make people smile, not cringe.

And don't assume this tip is addressed only to men. Women are engaging in this quickie jolt more often than ever.

Ross was jogging in Central Park when a woman driving past him on a motorcycle yelled out, "Hey, dude!" and roared off, laughing. Was Ross offended? Hardly. It made his day.

A recent Texas A&M study showed that men find women who flirt more attractive than women who don't. So be adventurous. Just be sure you're not giving anyone the wrong impression or engaging in the zipless flirt in an inopportune setting (walking through a tough part of town at two in the morning, for instance).

ADVANCED FLIRTING

When you're ready to move from the zipless flirt to more major interaction, consider the following flirting techniques.

Give someone a compliment. Relate it to a person, though--not an object. "I like your tie," leaves room for a man to wonder if you like the tie itself or him. Instead, try, "You look great in that tie; it brings out the blue in your eyes."

Show you're listening. Nod and add "uh-huh" every so often--hang onto the person's words for a second before jumping right in with a response. As you're probably aware, in one-on-one situations, the more you try to think of something to say, the more nervous you get. This is natural. During such lulls in the conversation, try going back to a subject you already talked about, instead of launching into a new topic. This shows you were paying attention and are interested in what was said, and re-engages the conversation. You don't always have to find a brilliant new topic to bring up.

Be helpful. If she mentions that her car is parked eight blocks away, offer to walk her there when she leaves later that night. Ask if you can carry a grocery bag for him if he's juggling more than one. Suggest a place to buy paint at a good price when she mentions she's about to paint her apartment (or offer your services with a brush). Show you're willing to extend yourself to get to know someone better, by helping to make his or her life a little easier.

Ask targeted questions. Don't stage an inquisition or get too personal. Pleasant queries like "Where did you grow up? or "Do you like scary movies?" will do. They show that you want to get to know the person. Avoid heavy issues and Big Questions such as "What's your life goal?"

Show an ongoing attraction. Mention that you saw him at the last dull convention, too. Bring up something she said in class last week. Tell him you love his new haircut. Tell her what you liked about the first time you heard her laugh.

Make eye contact. Hold someone's glance longer than a second, but don't stare. Look away and give the person time to register that the look was meant for them (and not for anyone else who might be around). Then do it again, and smile this time.

Execute the brush-by. Maybe there are twenty-two ways to get to the ladies' room. Take the one that puts him in your path. Walk in front of him so that he can see you. If it's crowded, you'll be able to brush by him innocently, without being obvious, and smiling as you pass.

Touch someone lightly. Briefly (and the brevity is the key here) put your hand on her arm during conversation. This is best after the person says something uncannily clever or amusing. The touch acknowledges you do indeed understand; you're in on the sentiment. But be careful not to overdo it.

Face the person you're flirting with. Don't give her your shoulder if you're seated side by side. Turn to face her while you're talking. It makes the other person feel more important.

Get close. You don't have to breathe on the knot of his tie, but don't stand three feet away, either. Disarm him by taking a step forward. And don't retreat.

STAY FLEXIBLE

These are merely suggestions, of course. Some work better than others in a given environment or with certain people. Find out which are most comfortable and most successful for you. Then develop your own flirting style. Once you do, don't keep it to yourself. Spread that charm around.

CHAPTER 43:
Send Someone
a Drink

Sending over a drink may seem cliche, but this simple gesture works--*if* you do it correctly. There are gentle and respectable ways to send someone a drink . . . techniques that will establish you as a thoughtful and potentially interesting person.

THE FIRST RULE

If you are drunk, go home.

While being drunk may help you to think you are relaxed, in actuality you may not be able to put your best foot forward. You may not be able to put *either* foot forward without falling on your face. Don't run the risk of a) making a fool of yourself, or b) getting in over your head with someone you've never met. Keep your wits about you and stay sober if you try the techniques in this chapter.

ESTABLISHING RAPPORT

When possible, try to establish a bit of rapport first. Look for some eye contact. If you get a smile or a full three-second look, that's a good sign that sending over a drink may be the next step toward conversation.

You can start with the drink if you prefer. When you see the waiter from the Intriguing Stranger's table come to the bar to pick up an order, just walk over and ask what that person is drinking. Then send another round. Be sure to include a drink for anyone sitting with the Intriguing Stranger (unless, of course, they appear to be romantically involved, in which case forget about sending over a drink).

Don't think that only men can send drinks. In fact, since men usually aren't prepared to receive drinks from women, they tend to be genuinely flattered by the gesture.

After sending the drink, wait ten minutes. Often, the Intriguing Stranger will thank you--either through a wave or a nod, or by coming over. Either response presents an opportunity for you to introduce yourself. If the Intriguing Stranger makes no contact, and ten minutes have gone by, you can saunter over and say hello.

This may feel a bit risky, but what the hell. The fact that the person didn't respond doesn't mean that he or she is not interested--or that he or she couldn't be interested.

Sometimes people get shy or nervous, and simply forget to thank the sender. Sometimes the waiter or waitress is busy, and gestures vaguely to a crowd to indicate the person who ordered the round, then rushes off to the next table.

When you walk over, the person will probably realize that you are the one who sent the drink. If this is not the case, *don't mention that you sent the drink*--at least not right away. You might sound like you're trying to buy the person's time. Just ask if you can join the table for a few minutes.

The "few minutes" provision is key here. Most people are willing to chance a couple of minutes, or at least engage in some conversation for a brief period. It's just for a few minutes--nothing overwhelming.

Keep the tone gentle and conversational. You will have to work harder at this in a bar because the atmosphere can be so intrusive. You may find yourself addressing Zen-like questions: how do you come on without coming on? But it can be done.

If the person is with a friend, talk to them both. Don't corner the one you like and exclude the one who doesn't interest you. Nothing will turn off the one you *do* like faster. Talking to both will allow the "pick-up" feeling to recede, and make you less of a threat. You'll be perceived as friendlier, put people at ease, and make a better impression.

THINGS YOU CAN START
THE CONVERSATION WITH

"How do you like this place?"

"Have you heard this band before? Isn't it good?"

"Have you heard this band before? Isn't it terrible?"

"Do you work around here?"

"I was having an argument with my boss today. It's really had me depressed all evening, and I'm thinking of quitting tomorrow if he and I can't work it out. Maybe you can help me. Do you remember if there were three Marx Brothers, or four?"

"What's the square root of 493?"

In other words, start the conversation with *anything*

but, "Do you come here often?"

You could say you noticed the Intriguing Stranger because he or she: was laughing; seemed to be having fun; seemed quiet; looked uncomfortable. You could ask the Intriguing Stranger if he or she: is celebrating something; is having fun; likes rock and roll; can hear anything over the noise. The idea here is to establish yourself as friendly, not predatory.

Remember, sending someone a drink does not entitle you to anything. You've made a nice gesture; that's all. If, for some reason, someone does not want to talk to you, *don't take the rejection personally*. It's the other person's loss. You don't have to tell the Steadily Less Intriguing Stranger that, but you should be sure to tell yourself.

A TIP ON TOOLS

Entrepreneur Diane Amsterdam has invented a singles helper called "meeting cards"; they're designed for use in brief encounters, when you're either pressed for time or too shy to initiate conversation. The cards are pre-printed with messages ranging from a simple "May I introduce myself?" to "I can't let you vanish into the crowd." Other favorites: "There is something about you that provokes me," and "You are beautiful; I am shy." On the back of each card is the legend "Call me." A space for your phone number is included.

If you don't like the idea of pre-printed messages, improvise. Write your own on the back of your business card or on a piece of paper. You can slip the message onto the tray of drinks the waiter brings, and instead of a phone number include your location at the bar. But be subtle here; when the waiter points you out, don't stand up suddenly, grin widely, and wave your arms around. Just smile politely and nod or raise your glass in a silent toast. The idea is to appear intriguing, not as though you're on fire.

CHAPTER 44:
Do Some Reality Testing

C arla learned something new about herself during a singles workshop she was taking. When asked to share with the group what actions she'd taken recently to enrich her social life, Carla launched into a long monologue, describing her every undertaking of the last week in merciless detail. The group began to grow restless, but the lecture went on; finally someone said, "Enough already!" This shocked Carla, but others in the group tried to get the message across in a supportive way. Even if her eventual point was an interesting one, the group had only so much time, and didn't want to spend it listening to Carla explain how she chose blouses. After some more discussion and encouragement from the group, Carla acknowledged that she'd never been aware of her tendency to drone on . . . but she *had* noticed that people kept "fading out" on her when she talked for some time. Men would come to her eager for conversation only to disappear into the restroom after a few minutes. Now she knew why.

Sometimes we're not the best assessors of our own strengths and weaknesses. Sometimes we can't pinpoint the causes of the difficulties that confront us. And sometimes, like Carla, we're completely oblivious to the fact that we even have a problem.

Try some reality testing with your friends and family to gain some insight on yourself. Ask someone you can trust if you can get some help in isolating what you do that you don't notice yourself doing.

THINGS THAT COULD BE
WORKING AGAINST YOU

Negative body language
Defensive comments
Questions that are too personal
Inappropriate requests
Shyness that's misinterpreted
Overpossessiveness
Speech that's too loud
Monologues instead of dialogues

At first, your friend might feel uncomfortable with this. He or she might dismiss your request and say you're terrific (which is true) and that it's impossible to come up with anything you could possibly improve on (which probably isn't true).

Tell your friend that you appreciate the support, but you'd like to be even *more* terrific. (And when your friend *does* start to make suggestions, don't get upset, angry, or defensive. Accept what's being said, and thank your friend for the honesty.)

At a pub on the way home from work, Jim met a woman who offered him her phone number before she left. When Jim got home, he called to make sure she got in safely. She told him that she really appreciated his concern, and said she looked forward to seeing him. The next day. Jim called just to say hello. She said it was nice to hear from him. The next day, Jim called to see how work was going. She seemed aloof. Two days (and two calls) later, she broke their first date with a lame excuse. Jim recounted the story to Mike, a friend of his. "You pestered her to death," Mike told him. "She probably figured that if you called that often before your first date, you'd expect her to wear a beeper if the two of you ever got involved."

Reality testing with a close friend does four important things.

One. It allows you to get accurate feedback about some easily changed behaviors that work against you--and maybe some not-so-easily-changed behaviors, as well.

Two. It enables you to offer the same positive support and feedback to others that they give to you. This will build your self-esteem and teach you how to be a better observer of behavior (including your own).

Three. It helps you realize that you are not alone in your "secret" concerns and worries. Everyone has vulnerabilities. Everyone feels insecure from time to time.

Four. It gives you the opportunity to confront things that get in your way and work to improve them--instead of merely dismissing them, or repeating the same "inexplicable" bad experiences endlessly.

Bill couldn't seem to make dates with women. He was a very funny guy--he had groups in stitches wherever he went. One night he asked his friend Sheila if she had any idea where he was going wrong. "But Bill," Sheila said, "everyone knows you're the funniest guy in the crowd." "A lot of good it does me," Bill answered. "Women don't like funny, apparently." Sheila looked at him for a moment. "That's really not true, you know," she said. "I *love* funny, and so do most of the women I know--but I like talking to someone, too. Did you know, Bill, that you haven't looked me in the eye once during this whole conversation?" Bill was stunned for a moment. "You're kidding," he said. "Nope," Sheila replied, "not for a minute. Maybe that's what the women you meet are reacting to--not your wonderful sense of humor. If you ask me, that's your biggest asset."

Rick was out with some friends from work; the discussion was hairstyles. One of the women in the group mentioned that a trip to the local salon was one of the best ways she knew to make herself feel desirable. Rick said, "You must be made of money. I've gone to the barber down the street for years--I've never spent more than $4.50 on my hair." "Yeah, and it looks it," someone piped in. Rick laughed, but later checked with a close friend to see if the criticism was on target. It was.

CHAPTER 45: Make the Call

I can't stand it anymore," Geena said at a recent singles workshop. "I give out my card. I'm personable. I'm warm. I'm everything I'm supposed to be--direct but not brash, aggressive but not overpowering, sexy but not sleazy. Still, men don't call me! Why on earth do they smile, strike up a conversation, take your card, and then never get back to you?" Larry, who was also attending the session that evening, bristled. "What do you mean? Why is it always *our* job to call? Why don't women ever call men?"

Let's not argue here about who really *should* make the call. The point is that opportunities are being passed over because, in too many cases, *the call is never made,* despite active interest from both sides!

WHY THE FIRST CALL WAS NEVER MADE--AND WHERE THE WOULD-BE CALLER WENT WRONG

What happened: George took Tina's number, but set it aside because he was busy at work. A few days went by. He picked up the number, thought of calling, but was called into a meeting unexpectedly that lasted all afternoon. That was Friday--and that weekend George had a date with someone else. A few more days went by. Before he knew it, George had let two weeks fly past. At this point, he was sure Tina would not remember him. He certainly didn't want to have a conversation like this:

"Hi, Tina. This is George. I met you at the Sullivan's costume party. George. No, it was a few weeks ago. You, ah, you gave me your card. Remember? It was, oh, about, nine-thirty, ten o'clock. I was dressed as Marc Antony, remember? The Sullivans. Martin and Elizabeth Sullivan."

So George never called.

Where George went wrong: He should have accepted the extremely low-level risk of a few uncomfortable moments on the phone. So what if he had to go through an awkward moment? In the grand scheme of things, we face greater risks than that when we cross the street in the morning!

After all, how many people are going to cross-examine you and demand that you explain why you waited so long to call? (Even if you do have to field such a question, you can just say you got tied up with a few things, but that you aren't tied up now!)

What happened: Lucy took Bill's number. Then she decided he lived too far away, and that she didn't want to date a pilot because they're always traveling. Lucy never called.

Where Lucy went wrong: Lucy is creating obstacles for herself--obstacles that could, with a little work, be overcome if the magic was there! Maybe there would be elements of the relationship that could compensate for the travel that's part of Bill's job. (Bill may even be able to arrange for free or discount passage for Lucy.) Maybe Bill could eventually switch to piloting commuter flights. Lucy might even learn she actually *enjoys* having stretches of time to herself. (After all, many successful couples incorporate such factors easily.) As it stands, Lucy will never find out.

What happened: Jeff took three numbers at the same party. He liked the first woman and decided not to call the others. But things with the first woman fizzled, and Jeff felt that too much time had passed to call the others. So he didn't.

Where Jeff went wrong: If the other women liked Jeff (and they did), they probably wouldn't care if he took a few weeks to call. And they certainly would have preferred that he call a few weeks after their first meeting to him not calling at all.

What happened: Leo felt Suzanne was nice, but he wasn't sure he really liked her enough to date her. Leo asked for Suzanne's number, but never called--because he couldn't decide if he wanted to start seeing her.

Where Leo went wrong: Sometimes, during that first, brief encounter, you can't easily tell if something nice might develop. But if you don't take the chance and make the call, you'll never find out. Many people, like Leo, aren't sure they're ready to ask the person out. So what? Call and make conversation, then see how you feel! There's no law that dictates that you *must* ask to go out with someone when you call!

Making a phone call is not the same as closing a deal, accepting a job, or signing a contract. It's okay to call someone just to talk, to ask how the day is going, or how a holiday was spent, or whether the person saw the last episode of that sitcom you both like. If it's been a while since your last contact, you can say that you've been tied up, but that you wanted the person to know you enjoyed your last meeting, and that you thought this call would give you the chance to say hello and chat.

Such calls are easy, non-threatening, and painless. They let you express your interest without pressure or any feelings of obligation. If things click, you'll probably both realize it. If you don't, you'll probably both know that, too. You may not always have enough information at a first meeting to know if the two of you can hit it off together. This type of call can give you the feedback you need.

THE ONLY GOOD REASON NOT TO MAKE THE CALL

The only good reason not to make the call is that you never asked for the other person's number to begin with.

Remember that you have that option during the first meeting. Don't feel pressured to ask for a number if you know things won't work out, just to be polite or (even worse) as a "bail-out" of a conversation that doesn't interest you.

If you're sure that under no circumstances will you go out with the person you're talking to, smile nicely, thank them for chatting, and say, "It's been nice to meet you."

Period. End of conversation.

Then move on.

If you simply can't face being that direct, tell a little white lie. Even if you hate lying, a white lie is better than asking for a phone number you don't want. You can excuse yourself to go to the rest room, to go look for your significant other, or to meet up with a friend you promised you'd meet.

A hint for women: many men really *like* women to call them. Our guess, based on discussions with seminar participants, is that there are more men out there who prefer that women make the initial call than there are women who feel comfortable doing so. That means there are a lot of men out there who would welcome a first call from a woman--but have rarely had the pleasure.

WHAT IF YOU CALL AND GET AN ANSWERING MACHINE?

Be prepared.

There are two schools of thought about dealing with answering machines. The first is never to leave a message if it's your first call--in other words, to hang up on the machine and call back until you get a live voice.

The second approach is to leave a message, but say that you're in and out a lot and that you'll try again. Then call back--but don't leave a message if you get the machine again. That way, you've let the person know that you tried, but you didn't babble on and on. Most people sound uncomfortable when they talk to a tape recorder.

Both methods are simple and painless, and will help you avoid coming off badly in an unexpected setting.

Reva met Michael at a party and took his number. When she called him, Reva was greeted by Michael's answering machine. She hadn't counted on such an eventuality, and the message she left confirmed the fact. Afterwards, Reva was not even sure she remembered to leave her number, but she thought Michael had it anyway. Michael never returned the call.

If you decide to leave a message, think about what you'll say *before you make the call.* Don't try to come up with something casual in the ten seconds you have before the beep. You'll end up stringing together a lot of pauses, "uh"s, and repetitions--even if you *were* captain of the college debating team.

CHAPTER 46:
Learn to Ask
for Less and
Get More

Alphonso met an attractive woman in a local pizza shop. She ordered a calzone; he asked how she liked it. The conversation progressed to more substantial topics, and Alphonso could tell that she seemed interested in him. When he asked whether she'd like to see a play with him, she hedged and said she wasn't sure; after all, she pointed out, she really didn't know him very well. Alphonso backed off immediately; he thought she was telling him she wasn't really that interested. He left the pizza shop without even asking for her phone number.

We've all had experiences with people who say one thing and mean another. But sometimes people really do mean what they say. The thought of spending an entire Saturday evening with a total stranger after having discussed nothing more revealing than a mutual preference for pepperoni could make anyone hedge.

One possibility is that the woman Alphonso met had just ended, or was just about to end, a serious relationship, and wasn't quite through the shock waves. If that were true, jumping into a romantic evening with a stranger would probably not be on her current top-ten list of What to Do on Saturday Night.

There are any number of other things that could have been runnning through her mind. They could include entries from the following non-exhaustive list.

"I hardly know him. Remember when I did that with Bernie? It was eight hours in hell."

"It's already Thursday. I don't want him to think I have no date for Saturday."

"I don't have anything I can wear to the theater-- unless the rules have changed and sweat pants are in."

"Is he married? Is he living with someone? He's not wearing a ring, but he hasn't said a thing about his personal life yet."

"Does he already have tickets? Did someone back out on him? What did she know that I don't?"

"Why is he asking me out on such an expensive date right away? If he's spending a lot of money on me, he probably expects something out of it."

HOW TO REACT TO HESITATION

The simple fact that someone is a little uneasy on your first encounter is *not* necessarily a sign that the person has no interest.

If you sense hesitation, ask for less and you might just get more. Maybe if Alphonso had suggested meeting at the pizza shop again--with the calzone on him--his new friend would have felt less threatened and said yes.

Of course, women run into the same wall when they ask men out, since men have many of the same concerns. In addition, they often face another hurdle: some men feel *they* should be doing the asking. They might not even know they feel this way. It may be an automatic response related to years of social conditioning.

These men will *always* hesitate when a woman asks them out, because they'll feel they've been placed in an awkward situation--even though they may know intellectually that there's no reason for the jitters. They probably don't *want* to feel uncomfortable when a woman asks for a date. They're certainly *glad* to know that the woman is interested. They just need a little help getting over the barrier of not being "in the driver's seat." Asking for less can work here, too.

When Carrie met Brandon at a tennis tournament, she thought he was interesting and wanted to get to know him better. But she wasn't sure how he'd react if she asked him on a date. In fact, Carrie didn't really know if she wanted to ask Brandon out for a fancy evening, but she did know she wanted to spend more time with him. When she told him about the monthly self-help lecture series she was attending, Brandon expressed interest. So Carrie invited him to join her at the next lecture; she said she had to work that day, but that she could meet him an hour or so before the lecture started. This gave the two of them enough time to chat, but it also provided Carrie with an out in case she felt uncomfortable.

All of this is not to say that you should avoid asking someone out for a night on the town. People do enjoy that experience from time to time, of course. You should be aware, though, that there are other ways of getting to know someone besides dinner and a movie (or dinner and an opera, for that matter).

Singles, both male and female, often complain about others who come on too strong. Such encounters can be intimidating, and may well scare your Intriguing Stranger off unnecessarily, even if your actions seem innocent enough to you.

If you're following old rules, rethink them. Perhaps your Uncle Nardo told you the "rules of the road" when you were 14: "If you like the girl, take her to dinner, take her to a show; just keep after her until she falls for you." Perhaps you never factored in that Uncle Nardo has now been married for 37 years to a woman who can't stand him. This isn't Uncle Nardo's life. It's yours. Think of new possibilities.

Gauge what you think the other person's reaction will be before you make *any* specific request relating to how you might get together again. Try saying, "I liked this conversation so much that I'd enjoy a replay." Then see how the other person reacts to the idea before you suggest anything. Maybe the Intriguing Stranger will actually suggest something! In any event, an approach like this will be less threatening; you will have expressed your initial interest, but allowed the other person a measure of control over the situation.

Asking for less is also a way to protect yourself. If you

think you're getting mixed signals, go slow. It hurts less when someone says no to a request to get together for coffee than when the same person turns down a request for dinner. And by minimizing your investment, you're also maximizing your potential for spending time with potential significant others.

CHAPTER 47:
Simply Smile

Dave is a big man with broad shoulders and bushy eyebrows. His friends know he's really the kind, sincere, friendly sort--but strangers walking down the street see a grave, gruff, don't-mess-with-me type instead. Since he doesn't usually see what his face looks like when he's out walking around, Dave never knew what impression he made on strangers. But one day a friend told him that she was a little intimidated by Dave when they first met; in fact, she said, he reminded her of a bear! But after she got to know him, she explained, she realized she'd been entirely wrong. His friend suggested that Dave try smiling more; when he smiles, his whole face lights up. His piercing eyes sparkle, his serious expression melts away, and he looks a lot more approachable

The problem with smiling more at people you don't know is that taking even such a small risk can cause anxiety. What if the person doesn't smile back? What if the person is already involved? What if you look like a weirdo? Such anxiety won't go away immediately, so don't give up if you feel it persisting.

The only way to make smiling a more natural action is to practice. Start by yourself in front of a mirror. (Even movie stars do this; it doesn't mean you're odd.) Then move to easy smiling targets: those in whom you have not invested the power to ruin your day if they don't respond in kind. Smile at people you'd never date, such as kids, married couples, a priest, or someone old enough to be your grandmother.

If smiling at potential dating prospects is still too scary, try smiling in a risk-free setting. Wait until you're off the bus and it's pulling away, or until the traffic light turns green, or until you're walking out of the restaurant. . . then flash a big toothy one at the person.

This works because you're not expecting a response, and because you won't be there to see if there is one.

You're still smiling for practice. After a while, you'll feel better about working your way up the ladder.

Stanley was reading *Barron's* while taking the bus to work. He noticed the lady across the aisle who was reading *Money*. Stanley kept alternating between glancing at her and skimming the paper. When she got up to leave, Stanley watched her get off the bus. From outside, she looked at him through the window and broke into a broad smile. Apparently she'd been watching Stanley, too, but he hadn't realized it!

One night as Freddie was leaving her apartment building on her way to yoga class, her doorman stopped her. "You know," he said, "whenever you smile at me, I know it's a real smile that comes right from your heart. You have no idea what it's like to stand here all day and watch people come and go. Many of them smile at me, but it's all in their lips. They pull them tight, curl them up, and think they're smiling. You're different, and I just want to thank you."

Where is the heart in *your* smile? Find it and don't be afraid to use it. People will notice the difference.

WHAT IF THEY DON'T SMILE BACK?

Sometimes you will be rejected no matter how high your smile's wattage. If you're aware that this is inevitable whenever you take risks, you may not feel as hurt when the rejections happen. You will be able to pick your smile up off the floor and use it again.

One rejection (or ten, or fifty) doesn't mean smiling is not worth taking the chance. And if smiling works even one time, you're in the black.

***

Marlene was in a sports bar the night of a big playoff game; there were about 20 men to each woman present. Marlene decided she would throw a smile to at least ten men. Across the bar, she saw a large fellow dressed in a tee-shirt and baseball cap, complete with little tufts of uncombed hair sticking out at all angles. He looked over and smiled. Marlene grinned back, and mentally reduced her target to nine. But the guy lifted his finger, pointed behind her, and said, "No. Not you. Her." She turned around to see a very pretty, much younger woman behind her. Even though she would never have gone out with the fellow in a million years, his reaction stung.

The best way to deal with the feelings such experiences dredge up is to talk about them. Share your rejection stories with close friends, and soon they'll be relating some of their own. You'll find that everyone encounters this sort of thing; it doesn't only happen to you.

Knowing that will make bouncing back easier, and you'll be more likely to keep at this smiling business. Eventually, smiling will produce less anxiety and more fun. You'll feel good making the effort, even when people don't return the grin. And when that happens, you won't think you've been rejected, because you weren't smiling to get anything in return. Smiling will just become part of who you are, an attractive part that will tell others you're friendly and approachable. You'll also reassure people that if they come over to strike up a conversation, *you* probably won't be issuing any rejections.

CHAPTER 48:
Read the Personals
and Place an Ad

About twenty years ago, there was a television saga set in the Old West about a lonely plainsman working a lumpy plot of land, gazing forlornly out toward the horizon, and drinking his own bad coffee every morning. He wrote to the local newspaper, asking them to run an ad along the following lines: "Mature cowboy seeks strong woman for companionship; ranch experience a plus."

Scene two: a thin, angular schoolteacher in a little red schoolhouse, surrounded by a bevy of rootin', tootin' underachievers, comes across the ad and circles it. Cut to: the schoolteacher bundled up and sitting on a train. Long shot: the lonely cowboy waits at the railroad drop-off, wearing an ill-fitting suit, preening himself, and looking agitated.

The train stops. The schoolteacher gets off. The cowboy looks at her. She looks at the cowboy. He takes her arm gently, and, without a word, they walk off into the wilderness.

Touching. But troubling. What if they discovered they couldn't stand each other? What if he was a light sleeper and she snored?

Ultimately, of course, none of that mattered. Theirs was a match borne of mutual need. No wine. No roses. No bull.

Modern romance may be somewhat different, but the personals are still an acceptable way for people who would never run into each other to, well, run into each other.

Some snickerers still believe personals to be a breeding ground for the bizarre, a haven for those inclined to spiked leather heels, whips and chains, and rubber clothing. Those who dismiss the personals section out of hand in this way are creating obstacles for themselves, and reinforcing their own negative mindsets. Although many people who use them don't find the love of their lives through the personals, virtually all are glad they placed the ad.

It's a fact: the personals can be your line into a significant number of single people whom you have not yet met. While they're not for everyone, they just might be for you.

Nate, a 40-year-old lawyer, recently placed an ad that received 160 responses. He's met his last three lovers through the personals over the past six years.

Maureen, a lively writer in her late thirties, got 50 responses for her ad. She called twenty of the men, actually met twelve, and continued to date three for a significant period.

Lizzie, an accountant, placed an ad that got right to the point. She said she wanted a family and kids. Guaranteed to scare men off, right? Wrong. She got 52 responses and dated one man for over a year.

Even if you never place or answer personal ads, just reading them can provide you with a great resource. Every time it seems that there is "no one out there" in your age range, or even your species, read the ads and you'll spot at least one person you might want to meet. Even if this person lives in Minnesota and you live in Maine, you'll probably get a morale boost and courage to carry on.

Once you become comfortable reading these ads, consider placing your own. This puts you in a dating frame of mind, maximizes your options, hones your social skills, and gives you something to look forward to. Placing a personal ad provides an element of mystery and adventure. After all, you never know who you might meet. And placing an ad gives you much more control than answering one does.

HOW TO GO ABOUT PLACING AN AD

Step One: Read the periodicals in your area and circle ads that grab your attention from both men and women. Save these in your singles clip file and review them. Try to figure out exactly what makes them so appealing.

Step Two: Write down what you really want to convey about yourself. Take some time to do this; things may pop up a few days after your first take pen in hand. Don't rush things. Play with phrases, but avoid cliches. (Do you know anyone who *doesn't* like long walks on the beach, candlelit dinners, and champagne?)

Step Three: Think of a hook. You want the first few words to grab someone and make them want to read on. "Attractive woman wants to meet . . ." will fade into obscurity the minute someone's eye passes over it. Better ideas run along the following lines:

> *Harpo speaks! . . . I'm the man your mother warned you about . . . Lily Tomlin looks, Sophia Loren soul . . . Recovering couch potato . . . Fiftyeverything . . . Romeostein, Romeostein . . . Rubensesque redhead . . . Man with accent . . . Lawyer with no defense . . . An older violin plays a sweeter tune . . . Looking for someone who knows the meaning of the word love and has the guts to answer this anyway . . .*

These hooks are not only entertaining, they're successful attention- grabbers. Instead of dryly describing the person who's placing the ad, they *show* something about the person by illuminating a few specific, key attributes.

Step Four: Now take all your ideas, underline those that are most important of all, and start to put the ad together. Don't be afraid to write too much; cutting is easier than adding. Keep editing and rewriting until you end up with a tight, sharp, and intriguing few lines.

Step Five: Read what you've written to friends of *both* sexes, especially of the sex you're trying to attract. Ask if the ad is an attention-getter, and if it gives an accurate picture of who you are. Make changes if you have to.

Step Six: Place the ad. Many people have no problem with steps one through five, but sputter to a halt here. "Cold feet" at this stage means you've wasted time, energy, and, most important, the potential for meeting someone interesting. Remind yourself that the worst thing that can happen is that you might not like the responses you get. In the unlikely event that this occurs, you need not respond to the letters you receive. Net loss: the cost of the ad.

Warning: do not make the two most common mistakes. The first is to be too restrictive about age ranges; the narrower you make your acceptable range, the fewer queries you'll receive. Don't miss out on opportunites unnecessarily. The second mistake is the catastrophic one of failing to mention the sex of the person placing the ad. (It really does happen, and it means extra time and expense once you decide to rerun the ad.)

CHAPTER 49:
Answer
an Ad

There are two theories on answering personals. The first would have you buy the periodical the day it hits the stand and answer the ad(s) of your choice immediately. The idea is that if someone is going to receive 160 answers to an ad, and yours comes in a week later than everyone else's, the person you want to reach will probably be married with six kids by the time your letter reaches its destination.

The second theory is that, in matters such as these, due consideration should always be given before responding. That berry-picker who lives in a log cabin upstate might sound perfect one day, but less promising a week later when you've had time to reflect on your priorities. Therefore, Theory Two goes, you should think things over-- and sleep on your decision--before responding impulsively to any ad.

Feel free to switch back and forth between the two, depending on your mood and your priorities. Fortunately, a few more clear-cut pointers about answering ads can help, as well.

HOW TO ANSWER IT

Cut out the ad and save it.   Having the ad in front of you when someone calls will remind you why you answered. This is especially important if you answer more than one ad at a time.

Keep your letter short and your response light.   Unless you're Wendy Wasserstein or Tom Wolfe, the odds are that a sixteen-page epistle isn't going to do much for you. Answer with a brief note--or perhaps your own mock ad. (*Not* the one you placed last week.)   A half-page if typed, or a full page if handwritten, ought to do it. If you say too much, you risk saying something that could be misinterpreted. Don't make your response look like a resume. Lengthy credits are for the end of "Gone with the

Wind."

When giving your phone number, mention the best time to reach you. Your prospective date may abandon ship after trying your number seven times and getting no answer.

Don't start having the relationship with the ad itself. This sets you up for rejection if the person doesn't call you. Send your response and forget about it.

Don't send an identical response to more than one ad. Julia and Melanie each placed ads in the same paper. They got several responses that were identical computer printouts! Only the box numbers had been changed. Touching, don't you think? Personalize each response you send by mentioning something specific that will let the person know why you chose his or her ad.

Do something to make your response stand out. Sue uses wildly colored paper. Joe sends a card, selected especially for the ad that caught his eye. Rhonda uses a deep yellow ink on dark paper.

WHAT HAPPENS WHEN SOMEONE CALLS?

Keep the conversation comfortable.

Don't ask a series of heavy questions or issue a list of demands. Feel free, however, to ask where the person lives, what they do for a living, or why they chose your response. These types of queries establish you as an intelligent, respectable person--and a legitimate potential date.

The first phone contact is where the multiple-response group can get into some touchy situations. Be careful: you should probably let the caller proceed under the assumption that the ad in question was the only one you answered. *Don't* say things like, "Oh, you're the one who moved here from Georgia." No one likes to feel like part of a crowd waiting for a date with you.

IF YOU MAKE PLANS TO MEET . . .

> . . . *always* pick a neutral, well-populated public setting.
> . . . *always* arrange for both parties to provide their own transportation.
> . . . *always* make the date for a cup of coffee, cocktail, or quick lunch.

. . . *always* agree on a way to identify yourself. "I'm 5' 8" with brown hair" will not do the trick. Better options: "I'll be wearing a fuchsia sweater"; "I'll be carrying a large blue book"; "I'll wear a white carnation."

WHAT SHOULD YOU EXPECT?

It's human nature to build a mental picture of someone from a voice on the phone. Remember, though, that the person you meet probably will not look anything like the image you have in your mind. Even if you are a little disappointed when you finally come face to face, give your date a chance. Don't let the disappointment of an unfulfilled fantasy get in the way of meeting someone wonderful.

WHAT TO DO ABOUT SECOND THOUGHTS YOU MAY HAVE

Your "gut instinct" is a wonderful barometer. It sends you little signals that can be invaluable. If, at any stage of the process, you get a funny, squeamish feeling in your stomach, take heed.

Remember that there's no law that says you have to meet with someone after the first phone conversation. If you're not sure you want to get together with the person who calls, ask if you can call back in a few days. This will give you time to think things over, and leave you in control of the situation. If you want, simply say, "I'm new at this, and I'd be more comfortable if we talked again before meeting."

If you've already set up a date, then decide a few days later that you don't feel right about meeting the person, call back and say something like, "I'm sorry, but I'm just not ready to get together yet." No matter what they say, stick to your decision.

In other words, if you decide that you don't want to meet someone, *don't.*

Of course, feeling unsafe or uneasy is not the same as simply feeling that your "fantasy lover" has not materialized. In the former case, you have an excellent reason not to meet someone; in the latter, you should consider loosening up a bit.

Bear in mind that even "bad dates" can lead to something interesting.

Greta had a fun phone conversation with Eric, a psychologist whose ad she'd answered. But when they met for a drink, she realized the spark was missing. To begin with, the "well-trimmed beard" he mentioned in the ad was more reminiscent of the Chicago Seven look. Differences in lifestyle and attitude that had not been apparent over the phone were painfully obvious in person. The conversation consisted of some remarks about the weather, an unexciting analysis of the restaurant's interior, and a whole lot of silence. The truth was obvious to both of them, and they were honest about the mismatch.

Two weeks later, Eric called Greta to tell her that he had a friend, Matt, who seemed to have much more in common with her. A day later, Matt called, and the two hit it off immediately. What's more, Eric got back in touch with Greta some weeks later, and asked if she'd like to join a singles group he was starting, a place where people could get together, share experiences--and, of course, keep an eye out for new and interesting date candidates!

It's a familiar injunction by this point, but do remember that *any* new person you meet is a potentially valuable addition to your singles network. There's no reason you can't use personal ads in this way, just as you use other methods to broaden your contacts.

WHAT TO DO IF, AFTER ANSWERING TEN PERSONAL ADS, YOU STRIKE OUT TEN TIMES

Answer number eleven. You have nothing to lose and everything to gain by using some persistence.

That advice may sound simplistic, but consider what Daphne did.

Daphne wanted to meet someone special--in fact, her real goal was to get married. She joined every dating service in town and answered innumerable personal ads. At the outset, when the dates turned into duds, she got discouraged. She gave herself time between the imperfect match-ups, then kept trying. She finally did get married . . . to the man she met in answering her 96th personal!

CHAPTER 50:
Find Out About Dating Services and Consider Using One

Just like the personals, dating services are a legitimate and time-proven method for meeting prospective mates. If you find yourself asking why you would ever stoop to using a dating service, feel free to borrow one of the following answers.

"WHY AM I JOINING A DATING SERVICE?"

"I'm going because I just moved here and dating services are the fastest way to get dates."

"I'm going because I recently ended a serious long-term relationship, and I'm not up to entering the dating scene again without some help."

"I'm going because I'm a risk-taker who enjoys the anticipation of meeting new people."

"I'm going because I'm not a risk-taker, and I want to meet someone with whom I'll have a better-than-average chance of success."

"I'm going because I'm so busy that I just don't have the time to do the work myself."

(After all, you eat take-out and send your laundry out, right?)

NOT A LAST RESORT

Using a dating service is a constructive way to meet people. It is not an act of desperation. At the very least, you should explore the options.

Dating services can vary widely in both price and focus. Four basic match-up methods exist. They are summarized briefly below.

Computerized services. These rely on a program to find other members who have similar interests or backgrounds based specifically on data fed into the computer. The computer doesn't interpret the data, as another person might; it just spits out people with matching data.

Hand matching. This relies on personal interviews, and often relies on intuition, as well as lists of attributes.

Video services. These organizations both tape you and allow you to match yourself by viewing tapes of prospective dates. You decide for yourself which videos to see, since you're using the service to view a pool of eligible singles. Payment is based on the number of tapes viewed.

Professional search agencies. These find a potential mate for you in much the same way as headhunters find executives to fill specific positions. They'll place ads, network for you, and generally give you VIP treatment.

HOW TO GO ABOUT
JOINING A DATING SERVICE

Read as much information about different dating services as you can find. Call to ask for a brochure. Don't get so involved in the sales pitch that you forget to ask about what's most important to you.

Prepare a list of questions to ask each service. How many active members does the service have in your age range and geographical areal? How long has the service been in business? What types and lengths of membership are offered? What are the fees for each? Does the service guarantee a certain number of dates, or offer refunds under certain circumstances? How long does it take for you to receive the first match? How long will you have to wait between matches? If you meet someone fabulous tomorrow morning, can you put your membership on hold? Add whatever other questions you feel are appropriate.

Pay attention to how the person recruiting you sounds and acts. Do you feel you trust this person to make a match?

Try to find someone who belongs to the service. Ask about his or her experiences there.

After you've called each service and had all your questions answered, make a choice based on the answers *and* on your gut instinct. If you really liked two services, consider joining both.

NOW WHAT?

If you are asked to go in for a personal interview, take it as seriously as you would a job interview. Imagine in advance what the setting will be like; picture yourself coming across as calm, witty, and clear. Dress well. Smile throughout, and be friendly. Use good body language and eye contact; be prepared to answer lots of background questions about your interests.

You might even want to bring some notes, so you won't get stuck or forget anything important. You'd be surprised at how many times dating service staff have to pull teeth to get people to admit to wanting to find someone with attributes beyond "sincere" and "nice." You'll find that being prepared for such questions will make you more relaxed and confident.

Remember that the quality of the service you get will depend, in large measure, on the quality of the interviews you give. These interviews may take the form of an oral interview, a series of forms for you to fill out, or both.

QUESTIONS YOU MAY ENCOUNTER
ON DATING SERVICE QUESTIONNAIRES

"Give a non-physical description of yourself."

"What characteristics do you find particularly objectionable in a prospective match?"

"What do you desire most--prestige, wealth, knowledge, power, or security?"

"How far will you travel for a date?"

"Do you wear glasses?"

"Do you have a physical handicap or a speech impediment?"

"Have you ever been confined to a hospital for the treatment of mental illness?"

"Have you ever been addicted to alcohol or drugs?"

"Have you ever been convicted of a felony?"

"List three references we can contact to verify some of the information given."

(Note: the nature of the organization is generally not revealed when refences are checked.)

You may well have to answer questions about height and weight. Everyone who uses the service has to answer the same questions. They are not designed to humiliate you. They are designed to help you get the best match.

In personal interviews, you should be aware of the interpersonal dynamics. Try to stand out from the crowd from the minute you walk in the door. Think of how many people your interviewer sees during the course of a day. Make sure you're one that makes an impression.

Ultimately, you want the interviewer to take a special interest in you--to want you to meet the best people the service has to offer. You won't get this by asking. You must show that you are a pleasant, cooperative, intelligent person who will make the interviewer look good for finding you.

WHAT TO DO IF YOU DON'T LIKE A MATCH

Give the service feedback. Be honest about what you didn't like. (And if you really hit it off with someone, be sure to tell the service what you *did* like.)

You can get discouraged easily if you had a bad match, and you may not want to talk about it, In this situation, however, you must; otherwise you may end up with a similar date in the future.

Someone the service refers to you may act completely different in a dating setting than in an interview. Don't get too angry over obvious duds. You want to get the most out of your membership, so be honest about your impressions and reasonable about complaints.

Joe loves kids; he wrote on his dating questionnaire that he was willing to meet women who already had children. His first match was a woman with ten kids. He called the service and amended his application to read that children were fine--but no more than five.

Warning for men: If you are a relatively attractive guy, you will probably get a lot of dates from a dating service-- maybe more than most women belonging to the same service. This is certainly nice, but the phenomenon has been known to overwhelm some; occasionally, a gentle soul finds himself turned into King Cad.

Don't fall victim to the kid-in-the-candy-store syndrome. Don't lose touch with the sensitive, non-manipulative, wonderful person you really are inside.

Epilogue: Staying Motivated

Now that you're making the effort to try some of the techniques in this book, you've probably had some surprising initial results (especially if you've been sitting at home since the autumn of 1982). You may be smiling at more people, becoming aware of opportunities you never noticed before, building more friendships, taking chances. Along the way, you're bound to have positive experiences. Enjoy them.

Getting motivated is the easy part. *Staying* motivated is the real challenge.

Of course, a big part of staying motivated involves being ready to learn. Congratulate yourself on a strong start in that area--otherwise how could you have made it this far in the book?

Some disappointments are inevitable. Although you can't prevent snags, you can prepare for them. The first step is to give yourself permission to hit a snag before you actually do--so that by the time you're in the throes of it, you won't add to your troubles by reinforcing a negative mindset. You'll just say, "Aha! I recognize this. It's a snag. It's just part of the process. It's no big deal."

Don't make a job out of finding and spending time with interesting people. Too many people "should" themselves half to death, telling themselves how they *should* be able to have a great time whenever they go out, or how they *should* be able to meet lots of people effortlessly.

This unnecessary pressure can actually lead to lower levels of motivation. If it won't be a perfect party (or date, or conversation), why bother? Don't buy into that game. Use the techniques we've outlined here as suggestions--not commandments. Have fun.

You don't have to "take action" all the time. You *can* hit a slump without losing all the motivation you've built up. Taking time out is perfectly acceptable. Sometimes, it's absolutely essential! Without slow periods, there's often no time for reflection and revisions of strategy. At worst, a slump is a temporary setback. At best, it is a well-deserved rest. What a slump is *not* is a good excuse to give up.

The following are some motivation maintenance techniques designed to shorten slump life. Using at least one motivator--whether you find it on this list or discover it on your own--is strongly recommended. Don't wait for hard times to try them. Take regular advantage of the boost you can receive from the ideas below. Some may not work for you, but, as with the other ideas in this book, you can be sure that *none* will work if all you do with this book is read it!

Go over your successes before you go out on a date, rather than playing the old tapes about all your failures. Consider writing down key phrases to help you remember the small success you might easily underestimate. Don't assume these successes have to be dating-related. Think about your last five really good times. Remember what pleasure they gave you. Let those positive feelings carry you out the door.

Set rewards for yourself. Tell yourself that after you've tried one of the ideas in this book, you'll buy yourself that snazzy pair of running shoes, or take the day off you've had coming for a month or two. Then stick to your bargain. The worst that could happen? You end up with a closet full of Nikes, or lower your stress level a few notches.

Repeat positive affirmations. Most bookstores sell audiotapes of "up" messages designed to help you relax, build your self-esteem, or reduce stress. Using them may help you recall your own strengths, and feel more positive when you're in difficult situations. You may even want to make your own affirmation tape.

Put a list of your attributes on your bathroom mirror (or just a note that says you're terrific)--so you'll see it and read it every morning. That way, you can concentrate on something constructive, rather than a mouth foaming over with toothpaste.

Make your own "power tape" of songs that really get your blood going. You know; the type that make you drum your fingers wildly on the steering wheel when they come on the radio, and make you sing backup even when you stop at a red light and the person in the car next to you is giving you funny looks. Each song you tape should be one that makes you feel you can do anything. Each should fill you with tremendous energy. Avoid at all costs the depressing numbers, or, even worse, "audio barbiturates" (the soulless, mind-numbing stuff they play on elevators). Then play the tape while you're getting ready to go out, or (even better) in the car on your way to meet someone.

Make a conscious effort to remind yourself that you aren't in this alone. You're now more prepared than ever to meet all the people you want to. Keep in mind that, in slow times as well as not-so-slow times, there are *always* lots of great single people out there who are looking. And you are one of them.

INDEX

Adult education classes, 138-140
Aerobics, 137
Alumni functions, 141-144
Art galleries and museums, 150-152
Auctions and sales, 103-104
Bars, misconceptions about, 70-71
    strategies surrounding visits to, 94-96, 160-162
Bookstores, 100-102
Brag lines, responding to, 128
Buddy system, advantages of, 79-81
Business cards, 23-26
Charitable organizations, 145-146
Cliche lines, responding to, 128-129
Co-workers, and dating, 30
Cocktail napkins, drawbacks of, 24
Conventions, 103-104
Conversation pieces, 19-22
Creative visualization, 63-66
Credibility, importance of, 59-62
Dancing, 136-137
Dating services, 187-191
Dealing with date "referrals," 33
Department stores, 97-99
Failure, importance of perspective with, 123-126
Family gatherings, 141-144
Feeling desirable, 27-29
Flirting, 156-159
Going out alone, 67-71
Health clubs, 147-149
Hesitation, dealing with, 171-174
Humor, dangers of inappropriate, 72-73
Humor, importance of, 72-74
Imagination, importance of, 63-66
Initiating conversation, 54-58
Jazz, 134-135
Jokes and stories, importance of, 72
Libraries, 100-102

Lines, learning how to take, 127
Mailing lists, 88-90
Making new friends, importance of, 75-78
Motivation, importance of, 192
Non-significant other parties, 130-131
Not trying, signs of, 45
Office, as dating resource, 112-115
Pacing oneself, importance of, 105-107
Percy, Walker, 123
Personal ads, 178-186
Pets, 91-93
    and where to walk them, 92-93
Professional organizations, 145-146
Projecting desirable image, 27
Reunions, 141-144
Ruts, how to avoid them, 108-111
Second chances, importance of, 43-46
Self-evaluation, 38-42, 163-165
Self-evaluation, 50-53
Sending someone a drink, 160-162
Shopping, 118-119
Short talk, 116-117
"Silly" secrets, 39-40
Singles clipping file, 86-87
Singles network, 30-33, 75-78, 112-115
Singles publications, 85-87, 178-186
Smiling, importance of, 175-177
Sports, 132-134
Taking oneself too seriously, dangers of, 50-53
Telephone calls, 166-170
Trade shows, 103-104
Transfering skills, 82-84
Trying too hard, signs of, 44
Type shifting, 34-37
Vacation "mindset," importance of, 120-122
Vacations, importance of, 153-155
Video stores, 100-102

Weddings, 141-144
Wish/need lists, 47
Workplace, as dating resource, 112-115

About the Authors

Sharyn Wolf is a consultant who has helped thousands of singles to meet the right people. She leads the successful workshops "50 Ways to Find a Lover" and "72 Ways to Flirt" as adult education courses. She is also a noted poet whose work has appeared in over thirty literary journals in the United States and Europe.

Katy Koontz has written for *The New York Times, The Washington Post, Playboy, Women's Day, Travel and Leisure,* and many other national publications. Before becoming a freelance writer, she was travel and features editor of *McCall's* and lifestyles editor of *Success.*

To

_____

From

_____

Broadstreet Publishing™
Racine, WI 53403
Broadstreetpublishing.com

Bible Promises for Teens
© 2014 by Broadstreet Publishing

ISBN 978-1-4245-4918-4

Compiled by Barbara Farmer
Cover design by Josh Lewandowski
Interior design by James Baker | www.jamesbakerdesign.com

Printed in the United States of America

BIBLE PROMISES

for Teens

BroadStreet
PUBLISHING

Contents

Alpha—God is the first place to go for all we need.....................................6
Abandonment 8
Abuse 10
Acceptance..12

Addiction 16
Anger...18
Beauty...20
Blessings 22

Commitment...26
Contentment...28
Courage..30
Creativity..32

Depression..36
Discouragement...38
Encouragement 40
Enthusiasm...42

Eternity..46
Faith..48
Faithfulness 50
Family..52

Fear...56
Forgiveness..58
Friendship..60
Generosity..62

Goodness..66
Grace..68
Grief...70
Guidance...72

Guilt...76
Health..78
Helpfulness...80
Hope...82

Humility...86
Identity..88
Inspiration 90
Integrity..92

Joy...96
Justice...98
Loneliness..100
Love...102

Money 106
Patience..108
Peace 110
Perseverance..112

Praise 116
Prayer..118
Promises 120
Purpose 122

Rebellion...126
Reconciliation...128
Respect..130
Salvation 132

Serving 136
Sexuality...138
Stress...140
Temptation 142

Thankfulness 146
Trust 148
Truth 150
Wisdom..152

Worry...156
Omega—God is the final answer for all we need....................158

Alpha

GOD IS THE FIRST PLACE TO GO
FOR ALL THAT WE NEED

"I am the Alpha and the Omega, the Beginning
and the End," says the Lord, "who is and who was and
who is to come, the Almighty."

REVELATION 1:8 NKJV

I fall to my knees and pray to the Father,
the Creator of everything in heaven and on earth.
I pray that from his glorious, unlimited resources
he will empower you with inner strength through
his Spirit. Then Christ will make his home
in your hearts as you trust in him.

EPHESIANS 3:14–17 NLT

Jesus Christ is the same yesterday and today and forever.

HEBREWS 13:8 NASB

God is the one who provides seed for the farmer and then
bread to eat. In the same way, he will provide and
increase your resources and then produce
a great harvest of generosity in you.

2 CORINTHIANS 9:10 NLT

My God will supply all your needs according to His riches
in glory in Christ Jesus.

PHILIPPIANS 4:19 NASB

Abandonment

Who shall separate us from the love of Christ? Shall trouble
or hardship or persecution or famine or nakedness
or danger or sword?... No, in all these things we are
more than conquerors through him who loved us.
For I am convinced that neither death nor life, neither
angels nor demons, neither the present nor the future,
nor any powers, neither height nor depth, nor anything
else in all creation, will be able to separate us from
the love of God that is in Christ Jesus our Lord.

ROMANS 8:35–39 NIV

If my father and mother leave me,
the LORD will take me in.

PSALM 27:10 NCV

Be strong and courageous, do not be afraid...for the LORD
your God is the one who goes with you.
He will not fail you or forsake you.

DEUTERONOMY 31:6 NASB

GOD made my life complete when I placed all the
pieces before him.... GOD rewrote the text of my life when I
opened the book of my heart to his eyes.

PSALM 18:20, 24 MSG

My God is changeless in his love for me,
and he will come and help me.

PSALM 59:10 TLB

Abuse

Don't be afraid, I've redeemed you.

I've called your name. You're mine.

When you're in over your head, I'll be there with you.

When you're in rough waters, you will not go down.

When you're between a rock and a hard place,

it won't be a dead end—

Because I am God, your personal God,

The Holy of Israel, your Savior.

I paid a huge price for you...

That's how much you mean to me!

That's how much I love you!

<small>Isaiah 43:1–4 msg</small>

The Lord is close to the brokenhearted
and saves those who are crushed in spirit.

<small>Psalm 34:18 niv</small>

You, O Lord, are a shield around me,
my glory, and the one who lifts up my head.

Psalm 3:3 nrsv

You are my refuge, a high tower where my enemies
can never reach me.

Psalm 61:3 tlb

My God in his steadfast love will meet me;
my God will let me look in triumph on my enemies.

Psalm 59:10 nrsv

The everlasting God is your place of safety,
and his arms will hold you up forever.

Deuteronomy 33:27 ncv

Acceptance

We have come to know and have believed the love
which God has for us. God is love, and the one who abides
in love abides in God, and God abides in him.
We love, because He first loved us.

1 JOHN 4:16, 19 NASB

Here I am! I stand at the door and knock. If anyone
hears my voice and opens the door, I will come in
and eat with that person, and they with me.

REVELATION 3:20 NIV

God is faithful, who has called you into fellowship
with his Son, Jesus Christ our Lord.

1 CORINTHIANS 1:9 NIV

How blessed is God!... Long before he
laid down earth's foundations, he had us in mind,
had settled on us as the focus of his love, to be made
whole and holy by his love. Long, long ago he decided
to adopt us into his family through Jesus Christ.
(What pleasure he took in planning this!) He wanted us
to enter into the celebration of his lavish gift-giving
by the hand of his beloved Son.

EPHESIANS 1:3–6 MSG

The Father gives me the people who are mine. Every one of
them will come to me, and I will always accept them.

JOHN 6:37 NCV

Addiction

Do you not know that your bodies are temples of the Holy Spirit, who is in you, whom you have received from God? You are not your own; you were bought at a price. Therefore honor God with your bodies.

1 CORINTHIANS 6:19–20 NIV

My child, listen and be wise:
Keep your heart on the right course.
Do not carouse with drunkards
or feast with gluttons,
for they are on their way to poverty,
and too much sleep clothes them in rags.

PROVERBS 23:19–21 NLT

You're blessed when you've worked up a good appetite for God. He's food and drink in the best meal you'll ever eat.

MATTHEW 5:6 MSG

Show me Your ways, O LORD;

Teach me Your paths.

Lead me in Your truth and teach me.

PSALM 25:4–5 NKJV

Now the Lord is the Spirit, and where

the Spirit of the Lord is, there is freedom.

2 CORINTHIANS 3:17 NRSV

I will teach you wisdom's ways

and lead you in straight paths.

When you walk, you won't be held back;

when you run, you won't stumble.

Take hold of my instructions; don't let them go.

Guard them, for they are the key to life.

PROVERBS 4:11–13 NLT

Anger

Always be willing to listen and slow to speak. Do not become angry easily, because anger will not help you live the right kind of life God wants.

JAMES 1:19–20 NCV

A gentle answer turns away wrath,
But a harsh word stirs up anger.

PROVERBS 15:1 NASB

Make sure it's all gone for good: bad temper, irritability, meanness, profanity, dirty talk. Don't lie to one another. You're done with that old life. It's like a filthy set of ill-fitting clothes you've stripped off and put in the fire. Now you're dressed in a new wardrobe. Every item of your new way of life is custom-made by the Creator, with his label on it.

COLOSSIANS 3:8–10 MSG

Get rid of all bitterness, rage, anger, harsh words,
and slander, as well as all types of evil behavior.
Instead, be kind to each other, tenderhearted, forgiving
one another, just as God through Christ has forgiven you.

EPHESIANS 4:31–32 NLT

People with understanding control their anger;
a hot temper shows great foolishness.

PROVERBS 14:29 NLT

Whatever is true, whatever is noble, whatever is right,
whatever is pure, whatever is lovely, whatever is
admirable—if anything is excellent or praiseworthy—
think about such things.

PHILIPPIANS 4:8 NIV

Beauty

Don't be concerned about the outward beauty of
fancy hairstyles, expensive jewelry, or beautiful clothes.
You should clothe yourselves instead with the beauty that
comes from within, the unfading beauty of a gentle and
quiet spirit, which is so precious to God.

1 Peter 3:3–4 nlt

You formed my inward parts;
You covered me in my mother's womb.
I will praise You,
for I am fearfully and wonderfully made;
Marvelous are Your works,
And that my soul knows very well.

Psalm 139:13–14 nkjv

The LORD does not look at the things people look at.
People look at the outward appearance,
but the LORD looks at the heart.

1 SAMUEL 16:7 NIV

Has anyone by fussing in front of the mirror ever gotten
taller by so much as an inch? All this time and money
wasted on fashion—do you think it makes that much
difference? Instead of looking at the fashions, walk out into
the fields and look at the wildflowers. They never primp or
shop, but have you ever seen color and design quite like it?
The ten best-dressed men and women in the country
look shabby alongside them.

MATTHEW 6:27–29 MSG

Blessings

You prepare a feast for me
in the presence of my enemies.
You honor me by anointing my head with oil.
My cup overflows with blessings.

<small>PSALM 23:5 NLT</small>

When you give a dinner or a supper, do not ask...
your relatives, nor rich neighbors, lest they also invite you
back, and you be repaid. But...invite the poor, the maimed,
the lame, the blind. And you will be blessed.

<small>LUKE 14:12–14 NKJV</small>

Oh, taste and see that the LORD is good;
Blessed is the man who trusts in Him!

<small>PSALM 34:8 NKJV</small>

The Lord bless you, and keep you;
The Lord make His face shine on you,
And be gracious to you;
The Lord lift up His countenance on you,
And give you peace.

Numbers 6:24–26 nasb

Do not repay evil with evil or insult with insult.
On the contrary, repay evil with blessing, because to this
you were called so that you may inherit a blessing.

1 Peter 3:9 niv

God's blessing makes life rich;
nothing we do can improve on God.

Proverbs 10:22 msg

Commitment

Commit everything you do to the LORD.
Trust him, and he will help you.
He will make your innocence radiate like the dawn,
and the justice of your cause will shine like the noonday sun.

PSALM 37:5–6 NLT

Let the beauty of the LORD our God be upon us,
And establish the work of our hands for us;
Yes, establish the work of our hands.

PSALM 90:17 NKJV

Work willingly at whatever you do, as though you were
working for the Lord rather than for people.

COLOSSIANS 3:23 NLT

Confirm God's invitation to you, his choice of you.
Don't put it off; do it now. Do this, and you'll have
your life on a firm footing.

2 PETER 1:10–11 MSG

Commit your work to the Lord,
then it will succeed.

PROVERBS 16:3 TLB

I have fought the good fight, I have finished the race,
I have kept the faith. From now on there is reserved for me
the crown of righteousness, which the Lord, the righteous
judge, will give me on that day, and not only to me but also
to all who have longed for his appearing.

2 TIMOTHY 4:7–8 NRSV

Contentment

● ● ● ● ● ●

If God gives such attention to the appearance of
wildflowers—most of which are never even seen—
don't you think he'll attend to you, take pride in you,
do his best for you? What I'm trying to do here is to
get you to relax, to not be so preoccupied with *getting*,
so you can respond to God's *giving*. People who don't know
God and the way he works fuss over these things,
but you know both God and how he works. Steep your life
in God-reality, God-initiative, God-provisions.
Don't worry about missing out. You'll find
all your everyday human concerns will be met.

MATTHEW 6:30–33 MSG

I have learned how to be content with whatever I have.
I know how to live on almost nothing or with everything.
I have learned the secret of living in every situation,
whether it is with a full stomach or empty,
with plenty or little. For I can do everything through Christ,
who gives me strength.

PHILIPPIANS 4:11–13 NLT

You're blessed when you're content with just who you are—
no more, no less. That's the moment you find yourselves
proud owners of everything that can't be bought.

MATTHEW 5:5 MSG

Courage

● ● ● ● ● ●

Be strong in the Lord and in his mighty power.
Put on all of God's armor so that you will be able
to stand firm against all strategies of the devil.
For we are not fighting against flesh-and-blood enemies,
but against evil rulers and authorities of the unseen
world, against mighty powers in this dark world,
and against evil spirits in the heavenly places.
Therefore, put on every piece of God's armor so you
will be able to resist the enemy in the time of evil.
Then after the battle you will still be standing firm.
Stand your ground, putting on the belt of truth and the
body armor of God's righteousness. For shoes, put on
the peace that comes from the Good News so that you
will be fully prepared. In addition to all of these, hold up
the shield of faith to stop the fiery arrows of the devil.
Put on salvation as your helmet, and take the sword
of the Spirit, which is the word of God.

Ephesians 6:10–17 nlt

Be of good courage,
And He shall strengthen your heart,
All you who hope in the Lord.

Psalm 31:24 NKJV

The Lord will keep you from all harm—
he will watch over your life;
the Lord will watch over your coming and going
both now and forevermore.

Psalm 121:7–8 NIV

May he give you the power to
accomplish all the good things
your faith prompts you to do.

2 Thessalonians 1:11 NLT

Creativity

In his grace, God has given us different gifts for doing
certain things well. So if God has given you the ability to
prophesy, speak out with as much faith as God has given
you. If your gift is serving others, serve them well.
If you are a teacher, teach well. If your gift is to
encourage others, be encouraging. If it is giving,
give generously. If God has given you leadership ability,
take the responsibility seriously. And if you have a gift for
showing kindness to others, do it gladly.

ROMANS 12:6–8 NLT

Go after a life of love as if your life depended on it—
because it does. Give yourselves to the gifts God gives you.
Most of all, try to proclaim his truth.

1 CORINTHIANS 14:1 MSG

There are different kinds of gifts,
but the same Spirit distributes them. There are
different kinds of service, but the same Lord.
There are different kinds of working,
but in all of them and in everyone
it is the same God at work.

1 Corinthians 12:4–6 niv

For we are God's masterpiece.
He has created us anew in Christ Jesus,
so we can do the good things
he planned for us long ago.

Ephesians 2:10 nlt

Depression

I keep asking that the God of our Lord Jesus Christ,
the glorious Father, may give you the Spirit of wisdom
and revelation, so that you may know him better.
I pray that the eyes of your heart may be enlightened
in order that you may know the hope to which he
has called you, the riches of his glorious inheritance
in his holy people, and his incomparably
great power for us who believe.

EPHESIANS 1:17–19 NIV

I will give them a crown to replace their ashes,
and the oil of gladness to replace their sorrow,
and clothes of praise to replace their spirit of sadness.

ISAIAH 61:3 NCV

No eye has seen, no ear has heard, and no mind
has imagined what God has prepared
for those who love him.

1 CORINTHIANS 2:9 NLT

I am the Light of the world; he who follows Me will not
walk in the darkness, but will have the Light of life.

JOHN 8:12 NASB

Praise be to the God and Father of our Lord Jesus Christ,
the Father of compassion and the God of all comfort,
who comforts us in all our troubles, so that we can comfort
those in any trouble with the comfort
we ourselves receive from God.

2 CORINTHIANS 1:3–4 NIV

Discouragement

● ● ● ● ● ●

In all this you greatly rejoice, though now
for a little while you may have had to suffer grief
in all kinds of trials. These have come so that
the proven genuineness of your faith—of greater worth
than gold, which perishes even though refined by fire—
may result in praise, glory and honor
when Jesus Christ is revealed.

1 PETER 1:6–9 NIV

Do not lose the courage you had in the past, which has a
great reward. You must hold on, so you can do what God
wants and receive what he has promised.

HEBREWS 10:35–36 NCV

We are pressed on every side by troubles, but we are not
crushed. We are perplexed, but not driven to despair.
We are hunted down, but never abandoned by God.
We get knocked down, but we are not destroyed.

2 CORINTHIANS 4:8–9 NLT

Let not your heart be troubled; you believe in God,
believe also in Me. In My Father's house are
many mansions.... I go to prepare a place for you.
And if I go and prepare a place for you,
I will come again and receive you to Myself;
that where I am, there you may be also.

JOHN 14:1–3 NKJV

Encouragement

Let everything you say be good and helpful, so that your
words will be an encouragement to those who hear them.

EPHESIANS 4:29 NLT

Remind the people...to be ready to do whatever is good,...
to be peaceable and considerate, and always
to be gentle toward everyone.

TITUS 3:1–2 NIV

Pleasant words are like a honeycomb,
sweetness to the soul and health to the bones.

PROVERBS 16:24 NKJV

Encourage one another and build each other up,
just as in fact you are doing.

1 THESSALONIANS 5:11 NIV

Those who hope in the LORD
will renew their strength.
They will soar on wings like eagles;
they will run and not grow weary,
they will walk and not be faint.

ISAIAH 40:31 NIV

You have been chosen by God himself—you are priests of
the King, you are holy and pure, you are God's very own—
all this so that you may show to others how God called you
out of the darkness into his wonderful light.

1 PETER 2:9 TLB

You, O LORD, are a shield around me,
my glory, and the one who lifts up my head.

PSALM 3:3 NRSV

Enthusiasm

Pay careful attention to your own work,
for then you will get the satisfaction
of a job well done, and you won't need to
compare yourself to anyone else. For we
are each responsible for our own conduct.

<small>GALATIANS 6:4–5 NLT</small>

Be wise in the way you act...;
make the most of every opportunity.
Let your conversation be always full of grace,
seasoned with salt, so that you
may know how to answer everyone.

<small>COLOSSIANS 4:5–6 NIV</small>

Work with enthusiasm, as though you were working for the Lord rather than for people. Remember that the Lord will reward each one of us for the good we do.

EPHESIANS 6:7–8 NLT

Dear friend, listen well to my words;
tune your ears to my voice.
Keep my message in plain view at all times.
Concentrate! Learn it by heart!
Those who discover these words live,
really live; body and soul....
Keep vigilant watch over your heart;
that's where life starts.

PROVERBS 4:20–23 MSG

I'm asking GOD for one thing, only one thing:
To live with him in his house my whole life long.
I'll contemplate his beauty; I'll study at his feet.

PSALM 27:4 MSG

For our light and momentary troubles are achieving for us
an eternal glory that far outweighs them all. So we fix our
eyes not on what is seen, but on what is unseen. Since
what is seen is temporary, but what is unseen is eternal.

2 CORINTHIANS 4:17–18 NIV

Before the mountains were brought forth,
or ever you had formed the earth and the world,
from everlasting to everlasting you are God.

PSALM 90:2 NRSV

We are citizens of heaven, where the Lord Jesus Christ lives. And we are eagerly waiting for him to return as our Savior. He will take our weak mortal bodies and change them into glorious bodies like his own.

PHILIPPIANS 3:20–21 NLT

I will come back and take you to be with me that you also may be where I am.

JOHN 14:3 NIV

Surely goodness and mercy shall follow me
All the days of my life;
And I will dwell in the house of the LORD
Forever.

PSALM 23:6 NKJV

Faith

Faith is confidence in what we hope for
and assurance about what we do not see.

HEBREWS 11:1 NIV

By entering through faith into what God has always wanted
to do for us—set us right with him, make us fit for him—
we have it all together with God because of our
Master Jesus. And that's not all: We throw open our doors
to God and discover at the same moment that he has
already thrown open his door to us. We find ourselves
standing where we always hoped we might stand—
out in the wide open spaces of God's grace and glory,
standing tall and shouting our praise.

ROMANS 5:1–2 MSG

Without faith it is impossible to please God, because
anyone who comes to him must believe that he exists and
that he rewards those who earnestly seek him.

HEBREWS 11:6 NIV

As many as received Him, to them He gave
the right to become children of God, even to those
who believe in His name.

JOHN 1:12 NASB

Through Christ you have come to trust in God. And you
have placed your faith and hope in God because he raised
Christ from the dead and gave him great glory.

1 PETER 1:21 NLT

Faithfulness

You must remain faithful to the things you
have been taught. You know they are true, for you know
you can trust those who taught you. You have
been taught the holy Scriptures from childhood, and they
have given you the wisdom to receive the salvation
that comes by trusting in Christ Jesus.

2 TIMOTHY 3:14–15 NLT

The steadfast love of the LORD never ceases,
his mercies never come to an end;
they are new every morning;
great is your faithfulness.

LAMENTATIONS 3:22–23 NRSV

Your love, Lord, reaches to the heavens,
your faithfulness to the skies.
Your righteousness is like the highest mountains,
your justice like the great deep.
You, Lord, preserve both people and animals.
How priceless is your unfailing love, O God!
People take refuge in the shadow of your wings.
They feast on the abundance of your house;
you give them drink from your river of delights.
For with you is the fountain of life;
in your light we see light.

Psalm 36:5–9 NIV

Family

Brothers and sisters, we ask you to appreciate those who
work hard among you, who lead you in the Lord and teach
you. Respect them with a very special love because of the
work they do. Live in peace with each other....
Be patient with everyone. Be sure that no one pays back
wrong for wrong, but always try to do what is good
for each other and for all people.

1 THESSALONIANS 5:12–15 NCV

You're blessed when you can show people how to cooperate
instead of compete or fight. That's when you discover who
you really are, and your place in God's family.

MATTHEW 5:9 MSG

Obey your parents in the Lord, for this is right.
"Honor your father and mother"—which is
the first commandment with a promise—
"so that it may go well with you and that
you may enjoy long life on the earth."

EPHESIANS 6:1–3 NIV

The father of godly children has cause for joy.
What a pleasure to have children who are wise.
So give your father and mother joy!
May she who gave you birth be happy.

PROVERBS 23:24–25 NLT

Fear

Even though I walk through the valley of the shadow of death,
I fear no evil, for You are with me;
Your rod and Your staff, they comfort me.
You prepare a table before me in the presence of my enemies;
You have anointed my head with oil;
My cup overflows.

PSALM 23:4–5 NASB

Steep yourself in God-reality, God-initiative,
God-provisions. You'll find all your everyday human
concerns will be met. Don't be afraid of missing out.
You're my dearest friends! The Father wants to give you
the very kingdom itself.

LUKE 12:31–32 MSG

Love has been perfected among us in this:
that we may have boldness in the day of judgment;
because as He is, so are we in this world. There is
no fear in love; but perfect love casts out fear.

1 John 4:17–18 nkjv

God has not given us a spirit of fear and timidity,
but of power, love, and self-discipline.

2 Timothy 1:7 nlt

The Lord is my light and my salvation—
whom shall I fear?
The Lord is the stronghold of my life—
of whom shall I be afraid?

Psalm 27:1 niv

Forgiveness

The LORD is compassionate and gracious,
slow to anger, abounding in love.
He will not always accuse,
nor will he harbor his anger forever;
he does not treat us as our sins deserve....
For as high as the heavens are above the earth,
so great is his love for those who fear him;
as far as the east is from the west,
so far has he removed our transgressions from us.

PSALM 103:8–12 NIV

If anyone is in Christ, he is a new creation; old things have
passed away; behold, all things have become new.

2 CORINTHIANS 5:17 NKJV

When you were stuck in your old sin-dead life,
you were incapable of responding to God. God brought you
alive—right along with Christ! Think of it! All sins forgiven,
the slate wiped clean, that old arrest warrant canceled
and nailed to Christ's cross.

COLOSSIANS 2:13 MSG

If we confess our sins, He is faithful and just to forgive us
our sins and to cleanse us from all unrighteousness.

1 JOHN 1:9 NKJV

Make allowance for each other's faults, and forgive anyone
who offends you. Remember, the Lord forgave you,
so you must forgive others.

COLOSSIANS 3:13 NLT

Friendship

There are "friends" who pretend to be friends,
but there is a friend who sticks closer than a brother.

PROVERBS 18:24 TLB

My command is this: Love each other as I have loved you.
Greater love has no one than this:
to lay down one's life for one's friends.

JOHN 15:12–13 NIV

The right word at the right time
is like a custom-made piece of jewelry,
And a wise friend's timely reprimand
is like a gold ring slipped on your finger.
Reliable friends who do what they say
are like cool drinks in sweltering heat—refreshing!

PROVERBS 25:12–13 MSG

Perfume and incense bring joy to the heart,
and the pleasantness of a friend
springs from their heartfelt advice.

PROVERBS 27:9 NIV

Two are better than one,
because they have a good return for their labor:
If either of them falls down,
one can help the other up.

ECCLESIASTES 4:9–10 NIV

The amazing grace of the Master, Jesus Christ,
the extravagant love of God, the intimate friendship
of the Holy Spirit, be with all of you.

2 CORINTHIANS 13:14 MSG

Generosity

Give, and it will be given to you.
A good measure, pressed down, shaken together
and running over, will be poured into your lap.
For with the measure you use,
it will be measured to you.

LUKE 6:38 NIV

One person gives freely, yet gains even more;
another withholds unduly, but comes to poverty.
A generous person will prosper;
whoever refreshes others will be refreshed.

PROVERBS 11:24–25 NIV

Remember this—a farmer who plants only a few seeds will get a small crop. But the one who plants generously will get a generous crop. You must each decide in your heart how much to give. And don't give reluctantly or in response to pressure. "For God loves a person who gives cheerfully." And God will generously provide all you need. Then you will always have everything you need and plenty left over to share with others.... Yes, you will be enriched in every way so that you can always be generous. And when we take your gifts to those who need them, they will thank God.

2 Corinthians 9:6–8, 11 nlt

Goodness

Look at those who are honest and good,
for a wonderful future awaits those who love peace.

PSALM 37:37 NLT

He has told you...what is good;
And what does the LORD require of you
But to do justice, to love kindness,
And to walk humbly with your God?

MICAH 6:8 NASB

Let us not become weary in doing good, for at the proper
time we will reap a harvest if we do not give up. Therefore,
as we have opportunity, let us do good to all people.

GALATIANS 6:9–10 NIV

Make sure you don't take things for granted and go slack in working for the common good; share what you have with others. God takes particular pleasure in acts of worship... that take place in kitchen and workplace and on the streets.

HEBREWS 13:16 MSG

Always pursue what is good both for yourselves and for all. Rejoice always, pray without ceasing, in everything give thanks.... Test all things; hold fast what is good.

1 THESSALONIANS 5:15–18, 21 NKJV

Keep your eyes focused on what is right, and look straight ahead to what is good.

PROVERBS 4:25 NCV

Grace

We are made right with God by placing our faith in Jesus
Christ. And this is true for everyone who believes,
no matter who we are. For everyone has sinned;
we all fall short of God's glorious standard. Yet God,
with undeserved kindness, declares that we are righteous.
He did this through Christ Jesus when he freed us
from the penalty for our sins.

ROMANS 3:22–24 NLT

He has saved us and called us to a holy life—
not because of anything we have done but because of his
own purpose and grace.

2 TIMOTHY 1:9 NIV

Since we have a great High Priest who has entered heaven,
Jesus the Son of God, let us hold firmly to what we believe.
This High Priest of ours understands our weaknesses, for
he faced all of the same testings we do, yet he did not sin.
So let us come boldly to the throne of our gracious God.
There we will receive his mercy, and we will find grace
to help us when we need it most.

HEBREWS 4:14–16 NLT

By grace you have been saved through faith, and this is
not your own doing; it is the gift of God—not the result of
works, so that no one may boast.

EPHESIANS 2:8–9 NRSV

Grief

God is the Father who is full of mercy and all comfort.
He comforts us every time we have trouble.

2 Corinthians 1:3–4 ncv

Dear brothers and sisters, we want you to know what will
happen to the believers who have died so you will not
grieve like people who have no hope. For since we believe
that Jesus died and was raised to life again, we also believe
that when Jesus returns, God will bring back with him the
believers who have died.

1 Thessalonians 4:13–14 nlt

Jesus said to her, "I am the resurrection and the life.
He who believes in Me, though he may die, he shall live."

John 11:25 nkjv

Now is your time of grief,
but I will see you again and you will rejoice,
and no one will take away your joy.

JOHN 16:22 NIV

He will wipe every tear from their eyes, and there will be
no more death or sorrow or crying or pain.
All these things are gone forever.

REVELATION 21:4 NLT

You're blessed when you feel you've lost what is
most dear to you. Only then can you be embraced
by the One most dear to you.

MATTHEW 5:4 MSG

Guidance

Trust in the LORD with all your heart,
And lean not on your own understanding;
In all your ways acknowledge Him,
And He shall direct your paths.

PROVERBS 3:5–6 NKJV

I'll take the hand of those who don't know the way,
who can't see where they're going.
I'll be a personal guide to them,
directing them through unknown country.

ISAIAH 42:16 MSG

When we obey him,
every path he guides us on is fragrant
with his lovingkindness and his truth.

PSALM 25:10 TLB

The LORD directs the steps of the godly.
He delights in every detail of their lives.
Though they stumble, they will never fall,
for the LORD holds them by the hand.

PSALM 37:23–24 NLT

I will instruct you and teach you in the way you should go;
I will counsel you with my loving eye on you.

PSALM 32:8 NIV

When you turn to the right or when you turn to the left,
your ears shall hear a word behind you, saying,
"This is the way; walk in it."

ISAIAH 30:21 NRSV

Guilt

Dear brothers and sisters, we can boldly enter heaven's
Most Holy Place because of the blood of Jesus.
By his death, Jesus opened a new and life-giving
way through the curtain into the Most Holy Place.
And since we have a great High Priest who
rules over God's house, let us go right into the
presence of God with sincere hearts fully trusting him.
For our guilty consciences have been sprinkled with
Christ's blood to make us clean, and our bodies
have been washed with pure water.
Let us hold tightly without wavering to the hope
we affirm, for God can be trusted to keep his promise.

HEBREWS 10:19–23 NLT

There is now no condemnation for those
who are in Christ Jesus, because through Christ Jesus
the law of the Spirit who gives life has set you free
from the law of sin and death.

Romans 8:1–2 niv

I, I am the One who erases all your sins, for my sake;
I will not remember your sins.

Isaiah 43:25 ncv

God did not send his Son into the world to
condemn the world, but to save the world through him.
Whoever believes in him is not condemned.

John 3:17–18 niv

Health

Praise the LORD, my soul,
and forget not all his benefits—
who forgives all your sins
and heals all your diseases,
who redeems your life from the pit
and crowns you with love and compassion,
who satisfies your desires with good things
so that your youth is renewed like the eagle's.

PSALM 103:2–5 NIV

Beloved, I pray that all may go well with you
and that you may be in good health,
just as it is well with your soul.

3 JOHN 1:2 NRSV

Are you hurting? Pray. Do you feel great? Sing.
Are you sick? Call the church leaders together to pray
and anoint you with oil in the name of the Master.
Believing-prayer will heal you, and Jesus will put you on
your feet. And if you've sinned, you'll be forgiven—
healed inside and out.

JAMES 5:14–15 MSG

My child, pay attention to what I say.
Listen carefully to my words.
Don't lose sight of them.
Let them penetrate deep into your heart,
for they bring life to those who find them,
and healing to their whole body.

PROVERBS 4:20–22 NLT

Helpfulness

Are your hearts tender and compassionate?
Then make me truly happy by agreeing wholeheartedly
with each other, loving one another, and working together
with one mind and purpose.

PHILIPPIANS 2:1–2 NLT

God is not unjust; he will not forget your work and the love
you have shown him as you have helped his people and
continue to help them.

HEBREWS 6:10 NIV

Let us consider how we may spur one another on
toward love and good deeds.

HEBREWS 10:24 NIV

"Lord, when was it that we saw you hungry and gave you food, or thirsty and gave you something to drink? And when was it that we saw you a stranger and welcomed you, or naked and gave you clothing? And when was it that we saw you sick or in prison and visited you?" And the king will answer them, "Truly I tell you, just as you did it to one of the least of these who are members of my family, you did it to me."

MATTHEW 25:37–40 NRSV

Carry each other's burdens, and in this way you will fulfill the law of Christ.... Therefore, as we have opportunity, let us do good to all people.

GALATIANS 6:2, 10 NIV

Hope

May the God of hope fill you with all joy and peace as you
trust in him, so that you may overflow with hope.

ROMANS 15:13 NIV

We can rejoice, too, when we run into problems and
trials, for we know that they help us develop endurance.
And endurance develops strength of character, and
character strengthens our confident hope of salvation.
And this hope will not lead to disappointment. For we
know how dearly God loves us, because he has given us
the Holy Spirit to fill our hearts with his love.

ROMANS 5:3–5 NLT

There is surely a future hope for you,
and your hope will not be cut off.

PROVERBS 23:18 NIV

In hope we have been saved, but hope that is seen
is not hope; for who hopes for what he already sees?
But if we hope for what we do not see,
with perseverance we wait eagerly for it.

Romans 8:24–25 nasb

The Lord is good to those whose hope is in him,
to the one who seeks him.

Lamentations 3:25 niv

God...rekindles burned-out lives with fresh hope,
Restoring dignity and respect to their lives—
a place in the sun!

1 Samuel 2:7–8 msg

Humility

Where you have envy and selfish ambition, there you find disorder and every evil practice. But the wisdom that comes from heaven is first of all pure; then peace-loving, considerate, submissive, full of mercy and good fruit, impartial and sincere. Peacemakers who sow in peace reap a harvest of righteousness.

JAMES 3:16–18 NIV

Those who accept correction gain understanding.
Respect for the LORD will teach you wisdom.
If you want to be honored, you must be humble.

PROVERBS 15:32–33 NCV

Humble yourselves in the sight of the Lord,
and He will lift you up.

JAMES 4:10 NKJV

In your relationships with one another,
have the same mindset as Christ Jesus:
Who, being in very nature God,
did not consider equality with God something
to be used to his own advantage;
rather, he made himself nothing
by taking the very nature of a servant,
being made in human likeness.
And being found in appearance as a man,
he humbled himself
by becoming obedient to death—
even death on a cross!
Therefore God exalted him to the highest place
and gave him the name that is above every name.

PHILIPPIANS 2:5–9 NIV

Identity

Take your everyday, ordinary life—your sleeping, eating,
going-to-work, and walking-around life—and place it
before God as an offering. Embracing what God does for
you is the best thing you can do for him. Don't become so
well-adjusted to your culture that you fit into it without
even thinking. Instead, fix your attention on God.
You'll be changed from the inside out. Readily recognize
what he wants from you, and quickly respond to it.
Unlike the culture around you, always dragging you down
to its level of immaturity, God brings the best out of you,
develops well-formed maturity in you.

Romans 12:1–2 msg

See what great love the Father has lavished on us,
that we should be called children of God!
And that is what we are!

1 John 3:1 niv

You did not receive a spirit of slavery
to fall back into fear, but you have received
a spirit of adoption. When we cry, "Abba! Father!"
it is that very Spirit bearing witness with
our spirit that we are children of God.

Romans 8:15–16 nrsv

Do everything without grumbling or arguing,
so that you may become blameless and pure,
"children of God without fault in a warped
and crooked generation." Then you will
shine among them like stars in the sky
as you hold firmly to the word of life.

Philippians 2:14–16 niv

Inspiration

I'm not saying that I have this all together, that I have it
made. But I am well on my way, reaching out for Christ,
who has so wondrously reached out for me.

PHILIPPIANS 3:12 MSG

Since we are surrounded by such a huge crowd of witnesses
to the life of faith, let us strip off every weight that
slows us down.... And let us run with endurance
the race God has set before us.

HEBREWS 12:1 NLT

I have come that they may have life, and that they may
have it more abundantly.

JOHN 10:10 NKJV

You are the light of the world. A town built on a hill cannot be hidden. Neither do people light a lamp and put it under a bowl. Instead they put it on its stand, and it gives light to everyone in the house. In the same way, let your light shine before others, that they may see your good deeds and glorify your Father in heaven.

MATTHEW 5:14–16 NIV

Pursue a righteous life—a life of wonder, faith, love, steadiness, courtesy. Run hard and fast in the faith. Seize the eternal life, the life you were called to, the life you so fervently embraced in the presence of so many witnesses.

1 TIMOTHY 6:11–12 MSG

Integrity

Don't let anyone look down on you because you are young,
but set an example for the believers in speech,
in conduct, in love, in faith and in purity.

1 TIMOTHY 4:12 NIV

The LORD grants wisdom!
From his mouth come knowledge and understanding.
He grants a treasure of common sense to the honest.
He is a shield to those who walk with integrity.

PROVERBS 2:6–7 NLT

A good name is to be chosen rather than great riches,
Loving favor rather than silver and gold.

PROVERBS 22:1 NKJV

The LORD detests lying lips,
but he delights in people who are trustworthy.

PROVERBS 12:22 NIV

The highway of the upright avoids evil;
those who guard their ways preserve their lives.

PROVERBS 16:17 NIV

Plant your seed in the morning and keep busy
all afternoon, for you don't know if profit will come from
one activity or another—or maybe both.

ECCLESIASTES 11:6 NLT

Love and truth form a good leader;
sound leadership is founded on loving integrity.

PROVERBS 20:28 MSG

Whoever pursues righteousness and love finds life,
prosperity and honor.

PROVERBS 21:21 NIV

Joy

He will yet fill your mouth with laughter
and your lips with shouts of joy.

JOB 8:21 NIV

This is the day the LORD has made;
We will rejoice and be glad in it.

PSALM 118:24 NKJV

Be truly glad. There is wonderful joy ahead....
You love him even though you have never seen him.
Though you do not see him now, you trust him; and you
rejoice with a glorious, inexpressible joy.

1 PETER 1:6, 8 NLT

May the God of hope fill you with all joy
and peace in believing.

ROMANS 15:13 NKJV

You shall go out in joy,
and be led back in peace;
the mountains and the hills before you
shall burst into song,
and all the trees of the field shall clap their hands.

ISAIAH 55:12 NRSV

Let all those rejoice who put their trust in You;
Let them ever shout for joy, because You defend them;
Let those also who love Your name
Be joyful in You.

PSALM 5:11 NKJV

The LORD has done great things for us,
and we are filled with joy.

PSALM 126:3 NIV

Justice

Whoever pursues righteousness and love
finds life, prosperity and honor.

PROVERBS 21:21 NIV

He will not judge by appearance, false evidence,
or hearsay, but will defend the poor and the exploited.
He will rule against the wicked who oppress them.
For he will be clothed with fairness and with truth.

ISAIAH 11:3–5 TLB

The LORD secures justice for the poor
and upholds the cause of the needy.

PSALM 140:12 NIV

The righteous care about justice for the poor.

PROVERBS 29:7 NIV

The world is unprincipled. It's dog-eat-dog out there! The world doesn't fight fair. But we don't live or fight our battles that way—never have and never will. The tools of our trade aren't for marketing or manipulation, but they are for demolishing that entire massively corrupt culture. We use our powerful God-tools for smashing warped philosophies, tearing down barriers erected against the truth of God, fitting every loose thought and emotion and impulse into the structure of life shaped by Christ. Our tools are ready at hand for clearing the ground of every obstruction and building lives of obedience into maturity.

2 CORINTHIANS 10:3–6 MSG

Loneliness

O LORD, You have searched me and known me.
You know my sitting down and my rising up;
You understand my thought afar off.
You comprehend my path and my lying down,
And are acquainted with all my ways.
For there is not a word on my tongue,
But behold, O LORD, You know it altogether.

PSALM 139:1–4 NKJV

You will search again for the LORD your God.
And if you search for him with all your heart and soul,
you will find him.

DEUTERONOMY 4:29 NLT

I will not leave you as orphans; I will come to you.

JOHN 14:18 NIV

"Though the mountains be shaken
and the hills be removed,
yet my unfailing love for you will not be shaken
nor my covenant of peace be removed,"
says the LORD, who has compassion on you.

ISAIAH 54:10 NIV

.

The LORD is near to all who call on him,
to all who call on him in truth.

PSALM 145:18 NIV

By this we know that we abide in Him and He in us,
because He has given us of His Spirit.

1 JOHN 4:13 NASB

Remember, I am with you always, to the end of the age.

MATTHEW 28:20 NRSV

Love

If I speak in the tongues of men or of angels,
but do not have love, I am only a resounding gong or a
clanging cymbal. If I have the gift of prophecy and can
fathom all mysteries and all knowledge, and if I have a
faith that can move mountains, but do not have love,
I am nothing. If I give all I possess to the poor and give
over my body to hardship that I may boast,
but do not have love, I gain nothing.
Love is patient, love is kind. It does not envy,
it does not boast, it is not proud. It does not dishonor
others, it is not self-seeking, it is not easily angered,
it keeps no record of wrongs. Love does not delight in evil
but rejoices with the truth. It always protects,
always trusts, always hopes, always perseveres.
Love never fails.

1 CORINTHIANS 13:1–8 NIV

God showed how much he loved us by sending his one and only Son into the world so that we might have eternal life through him. This is real love—not that we loved God, but that he loved us and sent his Son as a sacrifice to take away our sins. Dear friends, since God loved us that much, we surely ought to love each other. No one has ever seen God. But if we love each other, God lives in us, and his love is brought to full expression in us.

1 JOHN 4:9–12 NLT

Take nothing for granted. Stay wide-awake in prayer. Most of all, love each other as if your life depended on it. Love makes up for practically anything.

1 PETER 4:7–8 MSG

Money

Wealth from get-rich-quick schemes quickly disappears;
wealth from hard work grows over time.

PROVERBS 13:11 NLT

The one who sows sparingly will also reap sparingly,
and the one who sows bountifully will also reap
bountifully. Each of you must give as you have
made up your mind, not reluctantly or under
compulsion, for God loves a cheerful giver.
And God is able to provide you with every blessing in
abundance, so that by always having enough of everything,
you may share abundantly in every good work.

2 CORINTHIANS 9:6–8 NRSV

What good will it be for someone to gain the whole world,
yet forfeit their soul?

Teach those who are rich in this world not to be proud and
not to trust in their money, which is so unreliable.
Their trust should be in God, who richly gives us all we
need for our enjoyment. Tell them to use their money
to do good. They should be rich in good works
and generous to those in need, always being ready
to share with others. By doing this they will be storing up
their treasure as a good foundation for the future so that
they may experience true life.

Patience

As those who have been chosen of God, holy and beloved,
put on a heart of compassion, kindness, humility,
gentleness and patience.... Beyond all these things
put on love, which is the perfect bond of unity.

Colossians 3:12, 14 nasb

God is pleased with you when you do what you know is
right and patiently endure unfair treatment.

1 Peter 2:19 nlt

I appeal to you, brothers and sisters, in the name of our
Lord Jesus Christ, that all of you agree with one another in
what you say and that there be no divisions among you,
but that you be perfectly united in mind and thought.

1 Corinthians 1:10 niv

Wait patiently for the LORD.
Be brave and courageous.
Yes, wait patiently for the LORD.

PSALM 27:14 NLT

Be patient, then, brothers and sisters, until the Lord's coming. See how the farmer waits for the land to yield its valuable crop, patiently waiting for the autumn and spring rains. You too, be patient and stand firm.

JAMES 5:7–8 NIV

May the Lord lead your hearts into a full understanding and expression of the love of God and the patient endurance that comes from Christ.

2 THESSALONIANS 3:5 NLT

Peace

Since we have been made right in God's sight by faith,
we have peace with God because of what Jesus Christ
our Lord has done for us. Because of our faith,
Christ has brought us into this place of undeserved
privilege where we now stand, and we confidently
and joyfully look forward to sharing God's glory.

ROMANS 5:1–2 NLT

These things I have spoken to you, so that in Me
you may have peace. In the world you have tribulation,
but take courage; I have overcome the world.

JOHN 16:33 NASB

God is not the author of confusion but of peace.

1 CORINTHIANS 14:33 NKJV

Do not be anxious about anything, but in every situation, by prayer and petition, with thanksgiving, present your requests to God. And the peace of God, which transcends all understanding, will guard your hearts and your minds in Christ Jesus.

PHILIPPIANS 4:6–7 NIV

If people's thinking is controlled by the sinful self, there is death. But if their thinking is controlled by the Spirit, there is life and peace.

ROMANS 8:6 NCV

Blessed are the peacemakers, for they will be called children of God.

MATTHEW 5:9 NIV

Perseverance

Dear brothers and sisters, I have not achieved it,
but I focus on this one thing: Forgetting the past
and looking forward to what lies ahead,
I press on to reach the end of the race and
receive the heavenly prize for which God,
through Christ Jesus, is calling us.

PHILIPPIANS 3:13–14 NLT

Consider it pure joy...whenever you face trials
of many kinds, because you know that the testing of your
faith produces perseverance. Let perseverance finish
its work so that you may be mature and complete,
not lacking anything.

JAMES 1:2–4 NIV

Blessed is the one who perseveres under trial because, having stood the test, that person will receive the crown of life that the Lord has promised to those who love him.

JAMES 1:12 NIV

I waited patiently for the LORD;
he turned to me and heard my cry.
He lifted me out of the slimy pit,
out of the mud and mire;
he set my feet on a rock
and gave me a firm place to stand.
He put a new song in my mouth,
a hymn of praise to our God.
Many will see and fear the LORD
and put their trust in him.

PSALM 40:1–3 NIV

Praise

Because your love is better than life,
my lips will glorify you.
I will praise you as long as I live,
and in your name I will lift up my hands.
I will be fully satisfied as with the richest of foods;
with singing lips my mouth will praise you.

PSALM 63:3–5 NIV

It's who you are and the way you live that count before
God. Your worship must engage your spirit in the pursuit
of truth. That's the kind of people the Father is out looking
for: those who are simply and honestly *themselves* before
him in their worship. God is sheer being itself—Spirit.
Those who worship him must do it out of their very being,
their spirits, their true selves, in adoration.

JOHN 4:23–24 MSG

Sing to the LORD a new song;
sing to the LORD, all the earth.
Sing to the LORD, praise his name;
proclaim his salvation day after day.
For great is the LORD and most worthy of praise.

PSALM 96:1–2, 4 NIV

By Him let us continually offer the sacrifice of praise to
God, that is, the fruit of our lips, giving thanks to His name.

HEBREWS 13:15 NKJV

I will praise you forever, O God,
for what you have done.
I will trust in your good name
in the presence of your faithful people.

PSALM 52:9 NLT

Prayer

Ask and it will be given to you; seek and you will find;
knock and the door will be opened to you. For everyone
who asks receives; the one who seeks finds; and to the one
who knocks, the door will be opened.

MATTHEW 7:7–8 NIV

Love your enemies! Pray for those who persecute you!
In that way, you will be acting as true children
of your Father in heaven.

MATTHEW 5:44–45 NLT

I call on you, My God, for you will answer me;
give ear to me and hear my prayer.

PSALM 17:6 NIV

The Spirit helps us in our weakness. We do not know what
we ought to pray for, but the Spirit himself intercedes for us
through wordless groans. And he who searches our hearts
knows the mind of the Spirit, because the Spirit intercedes
for God's people in accordance with the will of God.

ROMANS 8:26–27 NIV

I urge you, first of all, to pray for all people. Ask God to help
them; intercede on their behalf, and give thanks for them.
Pray this way for kings and all who are in authority so that
we can live peaceful and quiet lives marked by godliness and
dignity. This is good and pleases God our Savior, who wants
everyone to be saved and to understand the truth.

1 TIMOTHY 2:1–4 NLT

Promises

Every good and perfect gift is from above, coming down
from the Father of the heavenly lights, who does not
change like shifting shadows.

JAMES 1:17 NIV

I am the vine; you are the branches. Those who remain
in me, and I in them, will produce much fruit.
For apart from me you can do nothing.... But if you remain
in me and my words remain in you, you may ask for
anything you want, and it will be granted!

JOHN 15:5, 7 NLT

All of God's promises have been fulfilled
in Christ with a resounding "Yes!"

2 CORINTHIANS 1:20 NLT

Not one word of all the good words which the LORD
your God spoke concerning you has failed;
all have been fulfilled for you.

JOSHUA 23:14 NASB

"For I know the plans I have for you," declares the LORD,
"plans to prosper you and not to harm you,
plans to give you hope and a future."

JEREMIAH 29:11 NIV

To him who is able to do immeasurably more than all
we ask or imagine, according to his power that is at work
within us, to him be glory...for ever and ever! Amen.

EPHESIANS 3:20–21 NIV

Purpose

What happens when we live God's way? He brings gifts into our lives...things like affection for others, exuberance about life..., a sense of compassion in the heart, and a conviction that a basic holiness permeates things and people.

GALATIANS 5:22–23 MSG

You make known to me the path of life;
you will fill me with joy in your presence.

PSALM 16:11 NIV

We know that all things work together for good to those who love God, to those who are the called according to His purpose.

ROMANS 8:28 NKJV

It's in Christ that we find out who we are and what we are living for. Long before we first heard of Christ and got our hopes up, he had his eye on us, had designs on us for glorious living, part of the overall purpose he is working out in everything and everyone.

Ephesians 1:11–12 msg

Don't you realize that in a race everyone runs, but only one person gets the prize? So run to win! All athletes are disciplined in their training. They do it to win a prize that will fade away, but we do it for an eternal prize. So I run with purpose in every step.

1 Corinthians 9:24–26 nlt

Rebellion

Because we belong to the day, we must live decent lives for all to see. Don't participate in the darkness of wild parties and drunkenness, or in sexual promiscuity and immoral living, or in quarreling and jealousy. Instead, clothe yourself with the presence of the Lord.

ROMANS 13:13–14 NLT

I am the LORD your God,
who teaches you what is best for you,
who directs you in the way you should go.
If only you had paid attention to my commands,
your peace would have been like a river,
your well-being like the waves of the sea.

ISAIAH 48:17–18 NIV

Once you were darkness, but now in the Lord you are light.
Live as children of light—for the fruit of the light is found
in all that is good and right and true.

EPHESIANS 5:8–9 NRSV

Keep your father's command
and do not forsake your mother's teaching.
Bind them always on your heart;
fasten them around your neck.
When you walk, they will guide you;
when you sleep, they will watch over you;
when you awake, they will speak to you.
For this command is a lamp,
this teaching is a light,
and correction and instruction
are the way to life.

PROVERBS 6:20–23 NIV

Reconciliation

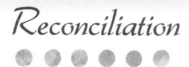

We have stopped evaluating others from a human point
of view. At one time we thought of Christ merely from a
human point of view. How differently we know him now!
This means that anyone who belongs to Christ has become
a new person. The old life is gone; a new life has begun!
And all of this is a gift from God, who brought us back
to himself through Christ. And God has given us
this task of reconciling people to him.

2 CORINTHIANS 5:16–18 NLT

You were separate from Christ...foreigners to the covenants
of the promise, without hope and without God in the world.
But now in Christ Jesus you who once were far away
have been brought near.

EPHESIANS 2:12–13 NIV

God put the world square with himself through
the Messiah, giving the world a fresh start by
offering forgiveness of sins. God has given us
the task of telling everyone what he is doing.
We're Christ's representatives. God uses us
to persuade men and women to drop their
differences and enter into God's work of
making things right between them.
We're speaking for Christ himself now:
Become friends with God;
he's already a friend with you.

2 Corinthians 5:19–20 msg

Respect

Appreciate those who diligently labor among you, and have charge over you in the Lord and give you instruction... esteem them very highly in love because of their work. Live in peace with one another.

1 THESSALONIANS 5:12–13 NASB

Live as free people, but do not use your freedom as an excuse to do evil. Live as servants of God. Show respect for all people.

1 PETER 2:16–17 NCV

Get the word out. Teach all these things.... Immerse yourself in them. The people will all see you mature right before their eyes! Keep a firm grasp on both your character and your teaching.

1 TIMOTHY 4:11, 15–16 MSG

Never let loyalty and kindness leave you!
Tie them around your neck as a reminder.
Write them deep within your heart.
Then you will find favor with both God and people,
and you will earn a good reputation.

PROVERBS 3:3–4 NLT

Have confidence in your leaders and submit
to their authority, because they keep watch over you as
those who must give an account. Do this so that
their work will be a joy, not a burden,
for that would be of no benefit to you.

HEBREWS 13:17 NIV

Salvation

Once you were dead because of your disobedience and your
many sins.... All of us used to live that way, following the
passionate desires and inclinations of our sinful nature.
By our very nature we were subject to God's anger,
just like everyone else. But God is so rich in mercy,
and he loved us so much, that even though we were dead
because of our sins, he gave us life when he
raised Christ from the dead.

EPHESIANS 2:1, 3–5 NLT

If you declare with your mouth, "Jesus is Lord,"
and believe in your heart that God raised him
from the dead, you will be saved.

ROMANS 10:9 NIV

What a God we have! And how fortunate we are to have him, this Father of our Master Jesus! Because Jesus was raised from the dead, we've been given a brand-new life and have everything to live for, including a future in heaven—and the future starts now! God is keeping careful watch over us and the future. The Day is coming when you'll have it all—life healed and whole.

1 PETER 1:3–5 MSG

For God so loved the world that he gave his one and only Son, that whoever believes in him shall not perish but have eternal life.

JOHN 3:16 NIV

Serving

Each of you should use whatever gift you have received to serve others, as faithful stewards of God's grace in its various forms. If anyone serves, they should do so with the strength God provides, so that in all things God may be praised.

1 PETER 4:10–11 NIV

Do you want to stand out? Then step down. Be a servant. If you puff yourself up, you'll get the wind knocked out of you. But if you're content to simply be yourself, your life will count for plenty.

MATTHEW 23:11–12 MSG

Even the Son of Man came not to be served but to serve others and to give his life as a ransom for many.

MARK 10:45 NLT

He who is greatest among you, let him be as the
younger, and he who governs as he who serves.
For who is greater, he who sits at the table,
or he who serves? Is it not he who sits at the table?
Yet I am among you as the One who serves.

LUKE 22:26–27 NKJV

You have been called to live in freedom,
my brothers and sisters. But don't use your freedom
to satisfy your sinful nature. Instead, use your freedom
to serve one another in love.

GALATIANS 5:13 NLT

Sexuality

This is my prayer: that your love will flourish
and that you will not only love much but well.
Learn to love appropriately. You need to
use your head and test your feelings
so that your love is sincere and intelligent,
not sentimental gush.

Philippians 1:9–10 msg

You say, "I am allowed to do anything"—
but not everything is good for you.
And even though "I am allowed to do anything,"
I must not become a slave to anything.

1 Corinthians 6:12 nlt

How can a young person stay on the path of purity?
By living according to your word.

PSALM 119:9 NIV

There's more to sex than mere skin on skin. Sex is as much spiritual mystery as physical fact. As written in Scripture, "The two become one." Since we want to become spiritually one with the Master, we must not pursue the kind of sex that avoids commitment and intimacy, leaving us more lonely than ever—the kind of sex that can never "become one."... In sexual sin we violate the sacredness of our own bodies, these bodies that were made for God-given and God-modeled love, for "becoming one" with another.

1 CORINTHIANS 6:16–18 MSG

Stress

Give your entire attention to what God is doing
right now, and don't get worked up about what may
or may not happen tomorrow. God will help you deal with
whatever hard things come up when the time comes.

MATTHEW 6:34 MSG

Be glad for all God is planning for you.
Be patient in trouble, and prayerful always.

ROMANS 12:12 TLB

You're blessed when you're at the end of your rope.
With less of you there is more of God and his rule.

MATTHEW 5:3 MSG

May the God who gives endurance and encouragement
give you the same attitude of mind toward each other
that Christ Jesus had.

ROMANS 15:5 NIV

Blessed is the one who trusts in the LORD,
whose confidence is in him.
They will be like a tree planted by the water
that sends out its roots by the stream.
It does not fear when heat comes;
its leaves are always green.
It has no worries in a year of drought
and never fails to bear fruit.

JEREMIAH 17:7–8 NIV

Temptation

If you think you are standing strong, be careful not to fall.
The temptations in your life are no different from what
others experience. And God is faithful. He will not
allow the temptation to be more than you can stand.
When you are tempted, he will show you a way out
so that you can endure.

1 CORINTHIANS 10:12–13 NLT

May God himself, the God of peace, sanctify you through
and through. May your whole spirit, soul and body be
kept blameless at the coming of our Lord Jesus Christ.
The one who calls you is faithful, and he will do it.

1 THESSALONIANS 5:23–24 NIV

I want you woven into a tapestry of love, in touch with everything there is to know of God. Then you will have minds confident and at rest, focused on Christ, God's great mystery. All the richest treasures of wisdom and knowledge are embedded in that mystery and nowhere else. And we've been shown the mystery! I'm telling you this because I don't want anyone leading you off on some wild-goose chase, after other so-called mysteries, or "the Secret."

COLOSSIANS 2:2–4 MSG

Thankfulness

Give thanks to the Lord, for he is good.
His love endures forever.

PSALM 136:1 NIV

Both riches and honor come from You,
And You reign over all.
In Your hand is power and might;
In Your hand it is to make great
And to give strength to all.
Now therefore, our God,
We thank You
And praise Your glorious name.

1 CHRONICLES 29:12–13 NKJV

Thanks be to God for his indescribable gift!

2 CORINTHIANS 9:15 NIV

Don't be drunk with wine, because that will ruin your life.
Instead, be filled with the Holy Spirit, singing psalms
and hymns and spiritual songs among yourselves,
and making music to the Lord in your hearts.
And give thanks for everything to God the Father
in the name of our Lord Jesus Christ.

EPHESIANS 5:18–20 NLT

We give thanks to God always for you, making mention of
you in our prayers; constantly bearing in mind your work
of faith and labor of love and steadfastness of hope.

1 THESSALONIANS 1:2–3 NASB

May you be filled with joy, always thanking the Father.
He has enabled you to share in the inheritance that
belongs to his people, who live in the light.

COLOSSIANS 1:11–12 NLT

Trust

I fall to my knees and pray to the Father,
the Creator of everything in heaven and on earth.
I pray that from his glorious, unlimited resources
he will empower you with inner strength through
his Spirit. Then Christ will make his home
in your hearts as you trust in him. Your roots
will grow down into God's love and keep you strong.
And may you have the power to understand,
as all God's people should, how wide, how long,
how high, and how deep his love is.
May you experience the love of Christ,
though it is too great to understand fully.
Then you will be made complete with all the
fullness of life and power that comes from God.

Ephesians 3:14–19 NLT

To you O Lord, I lift up my soul.
O my God, in you I trust.

Psalm 25:1–2 nrsv

The Lord is my strength and my shield;
My heart trusts in Him, and I am helped;
Therefore my heart exults,
And with my song I shall thank Him.

Psalm 28:7 nasb

You will keep him in perfect peace,
Whose mind is stayed on You,
Because he trusts in You.

Isaiah 26:3 nkjv

Truth

Jesus said to him, "I am the way, the truth, and the life.
No one comes to the Father except through Me."

JOHN 14:6 NKJV

Teach me your ways, O LORD,
that I may live according to your truth!
Grant me purity of heart,
so that I may honor you.

PSALM 86:11 NLT

Jesus said, "If you hold to my teaching, you are really
my disciples. Then you will know the truth,
and the truth will set you free."

JOHN 8:31–32 NIV

Truthful words stand the test of time,
but lies are soon exposed.

PROVERBS 12:19 NLT

Everyone who does evil hates the light, and will not
come into the light for fear that their deeds will be exposed.
But whoever lives by the truth comes into the light,
so that it may be seen plainly that what they have done
has been done in the sight of God.

John 3:20–21 NIV

Send out your light and your truth;
let them lead me;
let them bring me to your holy hill
and to your dwelling.

Psalm 43:3 NRSV

Open my eyes to see
the wonderful truths in your instructions.

Psalm 119:18 NLT

Wisdom

A wise man will hear and increase learning,
and a man of understanding will attain wise counsel.

PROVERBS 1:5 NKJV

Pay close attention, friend, to what your father tells you;
never forget what you learned at your mother's knee.
Wear their counsel like flowers in your hair,
like rings on your fingers.

PROVERBS 1:8–9 MSG

Wise words bring many benefits,
and hard work brings rewards.

PROVERBS 12:14 NLT

Wise men and women are always learning,
always listening for fresh insights.

PROVERBS 18:15 MSG

Cease listening to instruction...
And you will stray from the words of knowledge.

PROVERBS 19:27 NKJV

My child, never forget the things I have taught you.
Store my commands in your heart.
If you do this, you will live many years,
and your life will be satisfying.

PROVERBS 3:1–2 NLT

Teach the wise, and they will become even wiser;
teach good people, and they will learn even more.

PROVERBS 9:9 NCV

Wisdom is like honey for you:
if you find it, there is a future hope for you,
and your hope will not be cut off.

PROVERBS 24:14 NIV

Worry

Give all your worries and cares to God,
for he cares about you.

1 PETER 5:7 NLT

Do not worry about your life, what you will eat or drink;
or about your body, what you will wear. Is not life
more than food, and the body more than clothes?
Look at the birds of the air; they do not sow or reap or store
away in barns, and yet your heavenly Father feeds them.
Are you not much more valuable than they? Can any one
of you by worrying add a single hour to your life?

MATTHEW 6:25–27 NIV

Those who live in the shelter of the Most High
will find rest in the shadow of the Almighty....
Do not be afraid of the terrors of the night,
nor the arrow that flies in the day.
Do not dread the disease that stalks in darkness,
nor the disaster that strikes at midday....
If you make the LORD your refuge,
if you make the Most High your shelter,
no evil will conquer you;
no plague will come near your home.
For he will order his angels
to protect you wherever you go.

PSALM 91:1, 5–6, 9–11 NLT

Omega

GOD IS THE FINAL ANSWER
FOR ALL THAT WE NEED

Jesus stood and said..."Let anyone
who is thirsty come to me and drink.
Whoever believes in me, as Scripture
has said, rivers of living water will
flow from within them."

JOHN 7:37–38 NIV

Jesus...said, "For mortals it is
impossible, but not for God; for God
all things are possible."

MARK 10:27 NRSV

God can do anything, you know—
far more than you could ever imagine
or guess or request in your wildest dreams!

Ephesians 3:20 msg

I am the Alpha and the Omega—
the Beginning and the End.
To all who are thirsty I will give freely
from the springs of the water of life.

Revelation 21:6 nlt